The Lodge Officer's Handbook

For 21st Century Freemasonry

Bro.

James F. Hatcher III, P.M.

Presented to:

DEDICATION

This book is dedicated to all those brave souls who, when asked if they would be willing to serve from one to umpteen years in an Officer Chair in their Masonic Lodge, said, "Yeah, I guess so."

AND

To the Awesome Officers of "My Year in the East"

Bro. Mark Timothy Dixon, Our Senior Warden
Bro. Mark Timothy Webb, Our Junior Warden
Bro. Jason Aaron Deck, P.M., Our Treasurer
Bro. Michael Garland Weems, P.M., Our Secretary
Bro. Vernon William "Smokey" Peck, P.M., Our Chaplain
Bro. Dustin Emmit Wade, Our Senior Deacon
Bro. Garry Lee Wackerhagen, P.M., Our Junior Deacon
Bro. David Lee Williams, P.M., Our Senior Steward
Bro. James Justin Smith, Our Junior Steward
Bro. Frankie Joe Bounds, Our Faithful Tyler
Bro. David Edgar Williamson, P.M., Our Marshal
Bro. Joe Malcolm Mencer, P.M., Our Master of the Work
Bro. Carl Edward Reneau, P.W.J.G.D., Our Master Educator

And, our late Brother,

Bro. Lester Dean Steeley, Our Deputy Tyler
(Deceased while serving in Office)

CONTENTS

ACKNOWLEDGMENTS

Thanks goes out to all those Brethren, who assisted me through the chairs and providing much of the information, wisdom, and advice offered in this handbook.

Special thanks goes out to the following Brothers for the use of their herein referenced material, in part, in the writing of this handbook:

Grand Lodge of Tennessee, F.&.A.M.
M.W. Bro. Roy C. Etherton, G.M.
R.W. Bro. Michael D. Villines, Sr., G.S.
M.W. Bro. Thomas F. Boduch, P.G.M.

Grand Lodge of Maine, A.F.&.A.M.
M.W. Bro. A. James Ross, G.M.
R.W. Bro. Mark E. Rustin, G.S.
M.W. Wayne Adams, P.G.M.

Grand Lodge of Minnesota, A.F.&.A.M.
M.W. Bro. David E. Olson, G.M.
R.W. Bro. Douglas J. Campbell, G.S.
M.W. Bro. Neil Neddermeyer, P.G.M.

Grand Lodge of Virginia, A.F.&.A.M.
M.W. Bro. Wayne S. Flora, G.M.
R.W. Alan W. Adams, P.G.M. and G.S.
Bro. J. Mark Mills, P.M., Masonic Education Chairman

and to the

Masonic Lodge of Education for their Officer Job Descriptions.
(www.masonic-lodge-of-education.com)

INTRODUCTION

Masonic Lodge Officer Duties are solely dependent upon leadership.

Masonic Lodge Officers, as they move through the Masonic Officer Chairs, as in any organization, could not properly function without a leadership team which provides Masonic Officer Training. A successful organization's future depends upon how well this team of lodge officers work together to provide Masonic Officer training. In the business world, an organization is built around Presidents, Vice Presidents, General Managers, Regional Managers, Supervisors and Workers. Each position plays an important part in order for the organization to be profitable and successful. In essence, the Masonic Lodge Officer Duties and Masonic Officer Training structure, much like their counterparts in the business world, shoulder the Lodge Officer Responsibilities which makes a lodge successful.

Masonic Lodge Progressive Line: Lodge Officers are part of a "progressive line", which is also known as "going through the chairs" ...or as the Masonic Officer Chairs. This line of succession moves up one position at a time, generally, from one year to the next. If no one drops from the line, then theoretically, seven years from the time of becoming Junior Steward, the Master Mason will arrive at the Oriental Chair in the East as the Worshipful Master.

1

The progression is as follows: Junior Steward, Senior Steward, Junior Deacon, Senior Deacon, Junior Warden, Senior Warden...and then Worshipful Master. The progressive line is used in the United States and in many other jurisdictions, as well.

In the Masonic Lodge, the top five Lodge Officers are elected by the Lodge in the following order: the Worshipful Master, the Senior Warden, Junior Warden, Treasurer and Secretary are elected by the Lodge members at their annual elections. Normally each position is filled for one year, however they may be re-elected to the same position depending on the circumstance. Lodge elections are performed via a Masonic Ballot Box, and officers serve a term of office of one year.

The other officer chairs in the Lodge, which include the Senior Deacon, Junior Deacon, Senior Steward, Junior Steward, Marshal, Master of Ceremonies, Tyler and Chaplain are appointed positions by the Worshipful Master. Other members of the Masonic Lodge may be called on to serve on any of the numerous committees and/or special appointments at the will of the Worshipful Master.

The Lodge Officer duties and names of the officers are taken from very old customs dating back to the medieval stonemasons' guilds (one theory), and may extend as far back as the Roman Era with the Caementarii of the vexillationes of the College of Dionysian Artificers attached to the Roman Army Legions in England, during the 1st and Second Centuries A.D. (another theory).

The Apprentice System

To our ancient brethren, Freemasonry was composed of a series of moral lessons, conveyed by secret rituals, miracle plays, dramas, ceremonies, music and symbolism. These lessons were taught in spare time, on holidays, and in the evenings.

Ancient Lodges consisted of groups of men working on the erection of great buildings and edifices. In this process, they designed the structure, oversaw the construction, and educated young men in the arts, sciences, and morals. Being so educated in these disciplines, many became great masters of engineering and architecture, and their designs, many still standing, have stood the test of time and won the admiration or every age.

One can find a modern version of this system in our colleges of Architecture and Engineering, not in those who actually erect the buildings. In this manner our ancient brethren were students looking for a thorough education primarily in the seven liberal arts and sciences (Trivium and Quadrivium), and the of the Masters of the Lodges served as their teachers. Today, this segment of education has been replaced by the local school system.

The system of education used by our ancient Brethren was called the apprentice system. Young men of good character were entered in the Lodges as apprentices under the guidance of a Master known to be a good leader and teacher, generally for a period of seven years. The Master was not only responsible for the technical training of his apprentices, but was also responsible for their moral and spiritual development. This phase of education, developed in the ancient Lodges in a long and complicated system of lessons dealing with religion, history, and morality, is the part of their educational system that has been passed on to us and is what we now refer to as "Speculative Freemasonry".

As the young apprentices progressed in their training and developed their abilities, the more ambitious aspired to positions of leadership, much as young men do today. They then became candidates for the position of Master. To achieve this they studied and trained themselves, and in order to advance they presented a piece of work of their own design, completed under their own direction. This became known as their Master Piece. If it was accepted by the other Masters, and if their knowledge proved satisfactory and their work was "true," they were accepted as Masters. Once elected by the other Masters, they were then allowed to preside over Lodges of workmen, consisting of Apprentices entered onto the rolls as workmen, Fellows of the Craft (modern journeymen), and Masters, who had proven their workmanship.

Among our ancient brethren, the stonemason, who was not proficient in the lessons of architecture and engineering, was not allowed to learn the secret moral lessons of our Order, which distinguish it from other orders and have caused it to endure through the ages. Such Masons only worked in dry masonry, constructed without mortar. They were known as Cowans and never joined the Lodge. Men who have no sense of social duty, who have not learned to cement society with love, and who have no love for their fellow man can never understand Freemasonry.

We are the builders of spiritual edifices. During the course of our Masonic journey we will learn from those who have gone before us, and now will use that knowledge to make our world and ourselves a better place. Let us live our lives both privately and publicly in a manner that will inspire others, and let us realize that Freemasonry is a power today as in the past to build lofty character, to ennoble the mind, to purify the soul—in fact, to cause every man to travel the level of time upright and erect before God and our fellow man.

In England in the 1400s, under the reign of King Edward III, local city governments grew out of the merchant and craft industries in each city or town. After an operative Master stonemason created his "Master Piece" to the satisfaction of the Master of his craft, or guild, he was considered a "Master Mason". Heads of the guilds became heads of their town councils, mayors, sheriffs, etc. During this time, one of the ways which a local official proclaimed his rank was by wearing a badge of office, or jewel, on a chain around his neck. The practice is still in use today in England.

If you have ever watched a ceremony wherein a Lord Mayor (regular mayor in the United States) attends a formal ribbon cutting event, you would see an ornate necklace which is the medallion, signature of his office, around his neck.

Masonic Lodge Officers carry over this ancient guild tradition, today, in the form of the symbolic "jewels" of their offices.

Beginning Your Journey

The following advice has been adapted from the Grand Lodge of Maine's Lodge Officer Handbook. It is so well written, that any efforts to improve upon it would be hard to accomplish, and so we just state it to you, as they have so wisely stated it to their officers:

Freemasonry is a charitable, benevolent, educational and religious society. Its principles are proclaimed as widely as men will hear. Its only secrets are in its methods of recognition and of symbolic instructions.

It is charitable in that it is not organized for profit and none of its income inures to the benefit of any individual, but all is devoted to the promotion of the welfare and happiness of mankind.

It is benevolent in that it teaches and exemplifies altruism as a duty.

It is educational in that is teaches by prescribed ceremonials a system of morality and brotherhood based upon the Sacred Law.

It is religious in that it teaches monotheism, the Holy Bible is open upon its altars whenever a Lodge is in session, reverence for God is ever present in its ceremonial, and to its brethren are constantly addressed lessons of morality; yet it is not sectarian or theological.

It is a social organization only so far as it furnished additional inducement that men may forgather in numbers, thereby providing more material for its primary work of education, of worship, and of charity.

Through the improvement and strengthening of the character of the individual man, Freemasonry seeks to improve the community. Thus, it impresses upon its Members the principles of personal righteousness and personal responsibility, enlightens them as to those things which make for human welfare, and inspires then with that feeling of charity, or good will, toward all mankind which will move them to translate principle and conviction into action.

To that end, it teaches and stands for the worship of God; truth and justice; fraternity and philanthropy; enlightenment and orderly liberty, civil, religious and intellectual. It charges each of its members to be true and loyal to the government of the country to which he owes allegiance and to be obedient to the law of any state in which he may be.

It believes that the attainment of these objectives is best accomplished by laying a broad basis of principle upon which men of every race, country, sect and opinion may unite rather than be setting up a restricted platform upon which only those of certain races, creeds and opinions can assemble.

Believing these things, this Grand Lodge affirms its continued adherence to that ancient and approved rule of Freemasonry which forbids the discussion in Masonic meetings of creeds, politics or other topics likely to excite personal animosities.

It further affirms the conviction that it is not only contrary to the fundamental principles of Freemasonry, but dangerous to its unity, strength, usefulness and welfare, for Masonic Bodies to take action or attempt to exercise pressure of influence for or against any legislation, or in any way to attempt to procure the election or appointment of governmental officials onto influence then, whether or not numbers of the Fraternity, in the dictates of his conscience.

The information provided in this booklet is recommended for your consideration as you prepare yourself for the important duties as Master of your Lodge. It is our hope that the booklet will serve as a basis for the creation of an officer kit. One for each of the three principal officers of the Lodge. The outgoing Master would then pass his kit to the incoming J.W. at installation. This would provide a continuous link from one administration to the next, and might include items like the following:

- Grand Lodge Constitution
- Ritual

- The Master's Book - Claudy
- Guide - Masters & Wardens
- Candidates Lesson Books
- Evening Memorial Service
- Petitions
- Lodge Widows
- Updated List of Lodge Members
- Lodge By Laws

Brethren, you are approaching a great Masonic adventure. Soon you are going to manage the destiny of your Lodge. If you wish to become a good Worshipful Master, you must prepare yourself ahead of time. Many worshipful Masters have been heard to express this thought: "If I had another year to serve, I think I could do a real good job." If you hope to do a good job beginning in January, you must start to prepare for the task now.

The eyes of many will be upon you, first of all, your own Officers. You will be setting an example for them to follow. Watching also, the members of your Lodge. The verdict of these Brethren will determine Lodge attendance at future meetings. Your family and friends will either be proud of you, or sorry for you, depending on how well you do as Presiding officer of your Lodge. Many others you do not know will be watching and forming their opinions of Freemasonry by your performance as the head of your Fraternity in the community.

The office of Worshipful Master is the highest honor a Lodge can confer upon one of its Members. The Worshipful Master is the supreme ruler of his Lodge. If he is going to exercise that authority in a proper manner, he must be adequately prepared to do so. He should know in advance the duties of his office should not have to rely upon the Secretary for guidance.

Many helpful Masonic resources are available to you. However, you should read and become familiar especially with these - - I now call to your attention ;

First, the Constitution and Masonic Code of your Grand Lodge jurisdiction. As Worshipful Master, you cannot perform the duties of the office in a proper manner unless you know this book. In due time, each of you will swear to abide by the rules set forth in this volume. But how are you going to keep, support, maintain and abide by the provisions of the Constitution and Code, if you haven't read it and don't know what it's all about?

Next is the By-Laws Of Your Own Lodge. There should be no question concerning your Lodge's By-Laws that you could not answer without referring to this book.

The next book is the Holy Bible. Don't engage in a plodding cover to cover reading. Instead, read selectively. Your knowledge of this book, the Great Light in Freemasonry, should be well above average. You will be dealing with people. As Worshipful Master, you cannot afford to lose your temper nor to be annoyed by the many problems coin to all Lodges, There is no better textbook to teach you how to deal with people than the Holy Bible. Here you will find guidance, wisdom and strength.

As the Presiding Officer in your Lodge, you must have the ability to stand on your feet and talk effectively before people. This is not easy. It takes practice, experience and courage. Take every opportunity between now and the time of your installation to practice public speaking. This will lead to increasing success not only in Masonry but also in all, your other endeavors.

Here are a few suggestions to help you became a good public speaker. First, increase your vocabulary. We think in words, therefore, the more words at your command, the more lucid and effective your speaking. Words are tools of communication. Whenever you read or hear a word not familiar to you, look it up in a good dictionary. Study the correct pronunciation and if it fits into your vocabulary, use it.

Of the Seven Liberal Arts, give special attention to the first three: Grammar, Rhetoric and Logic. Grammar is the relationship of words to each other. Review your grammar. Eliminate careless speaking habits. You need good grammar to effectively express your thoughts.

Rhetoric is the art of speaking (or writing) with correctness and clearness. Read a book or two on rhetoric. It will improve your communication with your Lodge Members.

Logic is the science of reasoning. Think before you speak. Learn to express yourself in such a manner that your audience will understand what you are saying and will comprehend what you are talking about.

The practice of public speaking involves not only use of the voice, but also gestures, mannerisms, posture and general appearance. Reading aloud in a clear, distinct voice, enunciating every work is one good way to practice. Standing and speaking before a mirror will help you see how you look to the audience. Watch your feet, hands, posture, facial expressions and gestures. If you see something wrong, tell yourself about it. This method of self-criticism will help you eliminate bad habits which you see in that fellow looking at you from the mirror.

To each Senior and Junior Warden, the "Time is Now:" Yes, "Now is the Time" for you to make yourself ready for the hour and the day when you will occupy the Oriental Chair of your Worshipful Lodge.

Planning and designing interesting and appealing Lodge Meeting programs and activities takes time, thought and imagination. So, please do not "put off" to a later date the thinking and planning so necessary to put your "Master Plan" into action.

An excellent place to begin in planning and designing programs is the adoption of a "theme" for your "Year in the East." Your "theme" should be selected with the best needs and welfare of your Lodge in mind. By now, you should know the needs of your Lodge. So govern yourself accordingly.

As you begin constructing your programs for various months of the year, keep in mind the importance of "timing" and "arranging." Lay your stated Meetings out in front of you and then proceed to construct each stated Meeting program on its own. Some Lodge meeting programs do not lend themselves to certain times of the year. So, schedule certain programs when you feel they will be most effective and appealing. Yes, "timing" and "arranging" can be most important.

Once you have adopted your "theme" for your year and have finalized your overall program, you should decide on ways and means of communicating with your Lodge Membership. Communicating with the Craft is one of the most productive thing you can do. The finest Lodge Meeting programs and activities you can schedule will prove useless if you do not "include," "inform, "and "invite" the Members of your Lodge. "Getting the word out" to the Craft means doing it in "due time" so that the Member can schedule his time to attend and participate. Advance notice of upcoming events is so important. Last minute notices and announcements are practically useless.

How does a Worshipful Master or a potential worshipful Master communicate with the Craft? There are many ways. The Monthly Lodge Notice or "Trestle Board" is just one of many ways of communicating with the Craft. Special mailings of letters or flyers are effective. Telephone committees are also effective. And, by word of mouth through other Elective Officers and Appointive Officers and Committees to the general Membership. Yes, getting the work around is most important.

A final point on communicating covers that relationship between the officers and Members of the Lodge. It is a "sad state of affairs" when a Worshipful Master is not in open and free communication with his fellow officers and Members. Please do not permit this to happen.

A Symbolic Lodge cannot function in the true spirit of Freemasonry if any of the officers, Elective and Appointive, are "not on speaking terms with one another." Such a condition will definitely "mar the harmony and good order" so necessary for a Symbolic Lodge to function.

In your planning and preparation for your "Year in the East," make every effort to "tap" and use the talent within your own Lodge. So many Worshipful Masters seem to feel they must "go out of their own Lodge" and engage the services of other Master Masons. There are occasions when this is in order. However, it is recommended that you get acquainted with the hidden talent within your own Lodge and put it to use. Develop a Member's Talent Sheet...and actually use it.

Something good happens when a Brother is singled out to serve his Lodge, especially if he is not already serving as an Officer or on a Committee. As you review your Lodge Membership and get better acquainted with those Members living within a reasonable radius, you could very well find that you have "an acre of diamonds" in talent within your own Lodge. Review the file of Petitions and get to know the qualifications and specialties of your Numbers.

As Worshipful Master of your Lodge, one of the most important and lasting responsibilities you will have is that of appointing others to Floor Offices and various Committees. The future of your Lodge, and Freemasonry in your city may well depend on the Members you appoint to the various Floor Offices and the several Committees. Satisfy yourself that you are selecting and appointing the best qualified within your Lodge. Friendship should not influence such appointments. Many Lodges are suffering and in real trouble only because Members were appointed to an office in the Lodge who "just didn't have it," so to speak.

The Office of Worshipful Master is draped with honor, clothed with authority, cloaked with responsibilities and adorned with obligations. To the weak it lends strength. To the strong it teaches humility. To the faithful it offers an excellent opportunity to serve mankind.

While in your journey to occupy the Oriental Chair, read diligently all the information contained in this handbook. It is essential if you are to become a leader of man. Few men are born to preside in the East. You should arrive at that exalted station through diligent effort, preparation and service.

Finally, when you are duly elected and installed Worshipful Master of your Lodge, you must be Master in fact and not only in name. You must rule and govern your Lodge, taking up the work where your predecessor left off, and continue without hitch and without harm to the delicate fabric of human relationships which comprise a Masonic Lodge.

Be a leader and not a boss. There is a vast difference. There isn't one real problem within our Symbolic Lodges that couldn't be resolved by good leadership. For you, a future Worshipful Master of your lodge, the time is now. And, the Craft is anxiously waiting and depending on YOU:

Dale Carnegie, in his famous book "How to Win Friends and Influence People," says, "If you want to gather honey don't kick over the beehive." And then he mentions these road signs to follow:

1. Begin with praise and appreciation.
2. Call attention to people's mistakes indirectly.
3. Talk about your own mistakes before criticizing another.
4. Ask questions instead of giving direct orders.
5. Let the other man save his face.
6. Praise improvement.
7. Use encouragement. Make the fault seem easy to correct.

To master all the things mentioned as being Worshipful Master's requirements, and many more that have not been mentioned, seems like an insurmountable task. But you are reminded that countless thousands of Worshipful Masters have come and gone, some good and some not so good. Some have been outstanding in their Knowledge of and performance in that office. Some have been found wanting.

It is entirely within the power of any dedicated Mason to learn all this, and more. It depends on his desire, dedication, willingness and application.

In one or two years, your Senior and Junior Wardens will become Worshipful Masters of your Lodge. You and men like you, hold the future of Freemasonry in your hands. What are you going to do about it?

If a farmer wants a bountiful harvest in the fall, he doesn't loaf around at planting time in the Spring. If you want to reap a bountiful harvest for Lodge while you are its Worshipful Master, now is the time to do your planting. IT IS LATER THAN YOU THINK.

The following chapters will provide some of the information you will find helpful as you prepare yourself for the Honorable and Responsible office of a Worshipful Master and for other Masonic affairs. Do not discard this handbook. Read it, write in it, and learn from it.

Also, study and thoroughly learn the Masonic Funeral Service so you can conduct it in a solemn, skillful and impressive manner. It is the last time you will have the opportunity, in public, to pay your respects to a deceased Brother. Moreover, you are conducting a Masonic ceremony on one of the few occasions you will appear in public as Worshipful Master of your Lodge. For these few minutes, you and your Officers are under public scrutiny. Practice the Masonic Funeral Service and be ready for this important Masonic obligation.

Pay all due respects to your Past Masters. They are the bulwark of the Lodge. They are sincerely interested in their Lodge. But, sometimes some Past Masters became so interested that they attempt to run the Lodge for the Worshipful Master. When you become Worshipful Master of your Lodge, take every advantage of the experience, knowledge and advice of your Past Masters. Seek their counsel, but when all is said and done, make your own decisions. You are the Worshipful Master and the final responsibility for governing the Lodge is yours alone. Act in accordance with your best judgment as to what is best for your Lodge in particular and Freemasonry in general, ever the while remembering it is sometimes very lonely when you're at the top.

Brethren, I urge you to start now to prepare yourself for one of the most outstanding years of your entire life. Properly and thoroughly prepared, you will in time to come, look back on that significant year with justifiable pride and satisfaction. Each one of you has the potential to become the best Worshipful Master your Lodge ever had...period!

PROGRESSIVE LINE OFFICERS

1 THE JUNIOR STEWARD

The Junior Steward of a Masonic Lodge is an appointed officer of the Lodge. He is appointed by and can be removed at will by the Worshipful Master. He is tasked to understudy the Senior Steward position and fill in for the Senior Steward in his absence. The Junior Steward's principle role is to assist the Senior Steward and the Senior Deacon in the preparation of the Candidates.

The Jewel of his office is the Cornucopia, which is an exact duplicate to the Senior Steward's Cornucopia. The Cornucopia represents the "Horn of Plenty". It is a goat horn from antiquity filled with the "fruits of your labors" and represents a job well done. Like the Senior Steward, the Junior Steward carries a white Rod, topped with a cornucopia while at Labour in the Lodge.

Both the Senior and Junior Stewards carry rods, atop which are the jewels of their offices. The rods represent England's Lord High Steward's rod in the House of Lords.

The Junior Steward role in the Lodge is similar to that of an Assistant or Deputy Supervisor.

The following are the proposed duties of the Junior Steward, but may be amended by your Lodge By-laws, situation at hand, and the order of the Worshipful Master or the Wardens in his stead:

Suggested Duties of the Junior Steward

Check or fill in the Junior Steward's Duties in your Lodge.

❑ Arrive early. Assist the Deacons and other officers in performing their respective duties. See that the tables in the Dining Hall are properly furnished at Refreshment, and the Brethren are suitably provided for.

❑ Assist the Senior Steward in preparing candidates for their degrees and in other duties as necessary.

❑ Assume the responsibilities of the Senior Steward if he is not present.

❑ Notify the Worshipful Master and Senior Steward of all schedule conflicts and arrange for another Brother to assist the Senior Steward in that activity.

❑ Insure the cleanliness of the Kitchen and Dining Hall before leaving the Lodge. This includes, but not limited to:

BEFORE EVERY MEETING

(1)   Clean floors (Sweep and mop as necessary).

(2)   Ensure bathrooms are clean, replace toilet paper, refill paper towel holder and hand soap dispenser, if necessary.

(3)   Ensure salt & pepper and sweets caddies are filled and on the table before the meal is served.

(4)   Ensure napkins, flatware and drinkware are available.

(5)   Make coffee, both regular and decaf, and ensure there are

enough cups next to the coffee pot. If your Lodge uses disposable cups, use 8 oz. cups. There are some Brothers who drink coffee like water, but most will not. If you use 12 or 16 oz. cups, they will pour half of the cup of coffee out when it gets cold, and refill. Using the larger cups sizes for coffee will significantly increase your coffee expense and is unnecessary. Save your Lodge money and buy smaller cups for coffee.

AFTER EVERY MEETING

(1)   Proper storage of all consumables into sealed containers, if being kept. We have a day-use kitchen; there is no one to eat or drink leftovers in the middle of the night or next few days, so if the Brethren don't take it home-it generally goes into the trash at the end of the meeting or event.

(2)   Removal of all trash outside to trash cans.

(3)   Complete cleaning of all cooking utensils, pots and pans. Proper storage of such in cabinets, drawers, etc.

(4)   Complete cleaning of all counters, sink, appliances, and stove.

(5)   Clean floors (Sweep and mop as necessary).

(6)   Remove all soiled linen (wash and return at the next meeting). Set out clean linen for the next activity, if required.

(7)   Ensure bathrooms are clean, replace toilet paper, refill paper towel holder and hand soap dispenser, if necessary.

MONTHLY

(1)   Clean out refrigerators. (This includes a compete defrost if necessary.)

(2)   Complete cleaning of stove.

(3)   Scrub floor (mop and wax).

(4)   Clean up storage areas.

Other assigned duties:

❑   _____

_____

❏ _____

❏ _____

❏ _____

❏ _____

❏ _____

NOTES

In your Lodge you will have visiting Brethren. The Lodge may also, at times, be used by other appendant and concordant bodies, e.g., the Eastern Star, DeMolay, York and Scottish Rites, Shrine, Tall Cedars, Rainbow Girls, Aramanth, etc., as well as meetings and events by private parties and other community organizations. It is important that you continue to present a clean and wholesome place for the appendant bodies, visiting Brethren, and community members, who might just ask for a petition after using your facilities.

Preparing the Candidate

You should assist the Senior Steward in preparing the Preparation Room for the candidate's reception, prior to his admittance into the Lodge for his degrees. You should ensure that the candidate uniforms, hoodwinks, cable tows, and any other candidate paraphernalia are properly available and properly maintained at all times, to include laundering, repaired and/or replaced as needed or required. Assisting the Senior Steward, you should make the candidate feel welcome, calm any fears he may have, provide answers to any questions he may have prior to admittance (without any disclosure of the inner workings of the Lodge or degree work, of course), and ensure that the necessary questions are asked and satisfactorily answered, prior to the candidate gaining admittance into the Lodge.

Degree Work

As Junior Steward, you should learn the Senior Steward's part in the ritual work for all three degrees. You should attend as many degrees this year as you can, serving in the Steward Positions. Once you have mastered the Senior Steward's parts, then you should begin learning the Junior Deacon's part for the opening and closing parts of Stated and Called Meetings. You should also attend your Lodge's Practice Night with the Senior Steward, so that you can learn and improve on the floor work for the Stewards' positions in the degrees.

IF YOUR LODGE DOES NOT MEET FOR A REGULARLY SCHEDULED PRACTICE NIGHT, THEN SPEAK WITH YOUR MASTER AND WARDENS AND START ONE.

Steward's Festive Board Menu Planner

Date	Meal	Menu
1-15-13	JAN Stated Mtg	Shepherd's Pie, Green Beans, Dinner Rolls, Coffee, Tea, Apple Pie, Chocolate Cake

Steward's Festive Board Menu Planner

Date	Meal	Menu

Steward's Festive Board Menu Planner

Date	Meal	Menu

Steward's Festive Board Menu Planner

Date	Meal	Menu

Steward's Festive Board Menu Planner

Date	Meal	Menu

Degree Work as Junior Steward

Date	Degree	Part	Lodge
3-1-13	FC	JS	Masonic Lodge No 123 F&AM

Junior Steward Proficiency Checklist

Date Completed	Part Learned
	Junior Steward Degree Floor Work
	Senior Steward, 1st Section of EA Degree
	Senior Steward, 1st Section of FC Degree
	Senior Steward, 1st Section of MM Degree
	Senior Steward, 2nd Section
	Junior Deacon, Meeting Opening
	Junior Deacon, Meeting Closing

Practice Dates Attended as Junior Steward

Personal Notes as Junior Steward

Personal Notes as Junior Steward

2 THE SENIOR STEWARD

The Senior Steward of a Masonic Lodge is an appointed officer of the Lodge. He is appointed by and may be removed at will by the Worshipful Master.

The Jewel of his office is the Cornucopia, which is an exact duplicate of the Junior Steward's Cornucopia. The Cornucopia signifies the "Horn of Plenty". It is a goat horn from antiquity, filled with the fresh fruits and vegetables to denote the "fruits of your labors" and represents a job well done. The Senior Steward carries a white Rod, topped with a cornucopia while at Labour in the Lodge.

The Senior Steward is tasked to understudy the Junior Deacon's position and fill in for the Junior Deacon when absent. His principle role is to prepare the candidate(s) during ritual, assisted by the Junior Steward, escort them to the lodge room, and to assist the Senior Deacon as needed. In their entry Officer positions, both the Senior and Junior Stewards typically handle kitchen duties and wait staff for the members.

The Senior Steward's responsibilities are similar to that of a

Supervisor.

The following are the proposed duties of the Senior Steward, but may be amended by your Lodge By-laws, situation at hand, and the order of the Worshipful Master or the Wardens in his stead:

Suggested Duties of the Senior Steward

Check or fill in the Senior Steward's Duties in your Lodge.

❑ Arrive early. Assist the Deacons and other officers in performing their respective duties. See that the tables in the Dining Hall are properly furnished at Refreshment, and the Brethren are suitably provided for.

❑ Prepare the menu on a monthly basis for Called Meetings of that month and the next Stated Meeting and provide a copy of the menu to the Worshipful Master and Junior Warden. The Worshipful Master will advise and adjust the menu as appropriate. This information shall be presented at the monthly Officers' Meeting.

❑ Special Activities: The Senior Steward is responsible for the menu, procurement and preparation of materials for all special activities: including Saturday Morning breakfasts, picnics, fundraisers, and other special events as called by the Worshipful Master. Special committees may be formed to support the Stewards for these events.

❑ Provide a complete financial record of all activities and report them to the Secretary on a monthly basis (before each Stated Meeting).

❑ Oversee and administer the Kitchen Fund.

❑ Notify the Worshipful Master and Junior Steward of all schedule conflicts and arrange for another Brother to assist the Junior Steward in that activity.

❑ Insure the cleanliness of the Kitchen and Dining Hall before leaving the Lodge. This includes, but not limited to:

BEFORE EVERY MEETING

(1)   Clean floors (Sweep and mop as necessary).

(2)   Ensure bathrooms are clean, replace toilet paper, refill paper towel holder and hand soap dispenser, if necessary.

(3)   Ensure salt & pepper and sweets caddies are filled and on the table before the meal is served.

(4)   Ensure napkins, flatware and drinkware are available.

(5)   Make coffee, both regular and decaf, and ensure there are enough cups next to the coffee pot. If your Lodge uses disposable cups, use 8 oz. cups. There are some Brothers who drink coffee like water, but most will not. If you use 12 or 16 oz. cups, they will pour half of the cup of coffee out when it gets cold, and refill. Using the larger cups sizes for coffee will significantly increase your coffee expense and is unnecessary. Save your Lodge money and buy smaller cups for coffee.

AFTER EVERY MEETING

(1)   Proper storage of all consumables into sealed containers, if being kept. We have a day-use kitchen; there is no one to eat or drink leftovers in the middle of the night or next few days, so if the Brethren don't take it home-it generally goes into the trash at the end of the meeting or event.

(2)   Removal of all trash outside to trash cans.

(3)   Complete cleaning of all cooking utensils, pots and pans. Proper storage of such in cabinets, drawers, etc.

(4)   Complete cleaning of all counters, sink, appliances, and stove.

(5)   Clean floors (Sweep and mop as necessary).

(6)   Remove all soiled linen (wash and return at the next meeting). Set out clean linen for the next activity, if required.

(7)   Ensure bathrooms are clean, replace toilet paper, refill paper towel holder and hand soap dispenser, if necessary.

MONTHLY

(1)   Clean out refrigerators. (This includes a compete defrost if necessary.)

(2)   Complete cleaning of stove.

(3)   Scrub floor (mop and wax).

(4)   Clean up storage areas.

Other assigned duties:

❑ _____

_____

_____

❑ _____

_____

_____

❑ _____

_____

_____

❑ _____

_____

_____

❏ _____

_____

_____

NOTES

In your Lodge you will have visiting Brethren. The Lodge may also, at times, be used by other appendant and concordant bodies, e.g., the Eastern Star, DeMolay, York and Scottish Rites, Shrine, Tall Cedars, Rainbow Girls, Aramanth, etc., as well as meetings and events by private parties and other community organizations.

It is important that you continue to present a clean and wholesome place for the appendant bodies, visiting Brethren, and community members, who might just ask for a petition after using your facilities.

Preparing the Candidate

Assisted by the Junior Steward, you should see that the Preparation Room is prepared for the candidate's reception, prior to his admittance into the Lodge for his degrees.

You should ensure that the candidate uniforms, hoodwinks, cable tows, and any other candidate paraphernalia are properly available and properly maintained at all times, to include laundering, repaired and/or replaced as needed or required.

Assisted by the Junior Steward, you should make the candidate feel welcome, calm any fears he may have, provide answers to any questions he may have prior to admittance (without any disclosure of the inner workings of the Lodge or degree work, of course), and ensure that the necessary questions are asked and satisfactorily answered, prior to the candidate gaining admittance into the Lodge.

Steward's Festive Board Menu Planner

Date	Meal	Menu
1-15-13	JAN Stated Mtg	Shepherd's Pie, Green Beans, Dinner Rolls, Coffee, Tea, Apple Pie, Chocolate Cake

Steward's Festive Board Menu Planner

Date	Meal	Menu

Steward's Festive Board Menu Planner

Date	Event	Menu

Steward's Festive Board Menu Planner

Date	Meal	Menu

Steward's Festive Board Menu Planner

Date	Event	Menu

Steward's Festive Board Menu Planner

Date	Meal	Menu

SS's Lodge Supplies Inventory (First 6 Months)

Item	No. Req'd	Mon 1	Mon 2	Mon 3	Mon 4	Mon 5	Mon 6

SS's Lodge Supplies Inventory (First 6 Months)

Item	No. Req'd	Mon 1	Mon 2	Mon 3	Mon 4	Mon 5	Mon 6

SS's Lodge Supplies Inventory (First 6 Months)

Item	No. Req'd	Mon 1	Mon 2	Mon 3	Mon 4	Mon 5	Mon 6

SS's Lodge Supplies Inventory (Last 6 Months)

Item	No. Req'd	Mon 7	Mon 8	Mon 9	Mon 10	Mon 11	Mon 12

SS's Lodge Supplies Inventory (Last 6 Months)

Item	No. Req'd	Mon 7	Mon 8	Mon 9	Mon 10	Mon 11	Mon 12

SS's Lodge Supplies Inventory (Last 6 Months)

Item	No. Req'd	Mon 7	Mon 8	Mon 9	Mon 10	Mon 11	Mon 12

Degree Work

As Senior Steward, you should learn the Senior Steward's part in the ritual work for all three degrees. You should attend as many degrees this year as you can, serving in the Steward Positions.

Once you have mastered the Senior Steward's parts, then you should begin learning the Junior Deacon's part for the opening and closing parts of Stated and Called Meetings. If you have the time to learn it, you should then start working on learning the Senior Deacon's parts for meetings. You should also attend your Lodge's Practice Night with the Junior Steward, so that you can learn and improve on the floor work for the Stewards' positions in the degrees. IF YOUR LODGE DOES NOT MEET FOR A REGULARLY SCHEDULED PRACTICE NIGHT, THEN SPEAK WITH YOUR MASTER AND WARDENS AND START ONE.

Senior Steward Proficiency Checklist

Date Completed	Part Learned
	Junior Steward Degree Floor Work
	Senior Steward, 1st Section of EA Degree
	Senior Steward, 1st Section of FC Degree
	Senior Steward, 1st Section of MM Degree
	Senior Steward, 2nd Section
	Junior Deacon, Meeting Opening
	Junior Deacon, Meeting Closing
	Senior Deacon, Meeting Opening
	Senior Deacon, Meeting Closing

Degree Work as Senior Steward

Date	Degree	Part	Lodge
3-1-13	EA	SS	Masonic Lodge No 357 AF&AM

Personal Notes as Senior Steward

Personal Notes as Senior Steward

Personal Notes as Senior Steward

_____

_____

_____

_____

_____

_____

_____

_____

_____

_____

_____

_____

_____

_____

_____

_____

_____

3 JUNIOR DEACON

The Junior Deacon of a Masonic Lodge is an assistant officer of the Lodge. He sits to the lower right of the Senior Warden, and is appointed by and can be removed at will by the Worshipful Master. Like his senior counterpart, the Senior Deacon, the Jewel of his office is the Square and Compass, however the Junior Deacon's Square and Compass has a moon in the center (rather than a sun), which signifies that he is in the West. The Junior Deacon carries a blue Staff, topped with a moon emblem inside the Square and Compasses while at Labour in the Lodge.

The Junior Deacon's principle roles are to assist the Senior Warden by carrying messages from the Senior Warden in the West to the Junior Warden in the South and to guard the inner door of the Lodge. It is his duty to ascertain at all times whether the Tyler is guarding the door and only allowing visitors to enter after they have been properly vouched for. The Junior Deacon and the Tyler communicate with each other by knocking on the door (the Tyler from the outside...and the Junior Deacon from the inside). Some jurisdictions split this position into two positions...that of the Junior Deacon and the Inner Guard. Most jurisdictions do not.

The Junior Deacon's position is similar to a Manager.

The following are the proposed duties of the Junior Deacon, but may be amended by your Lodge By-laws, situation at hand, and the order of the Worshipful Master or the Wardens in his stead:

Suggested Duties of the Junior Deacon

Check or fill in the Junior Deacon's Duties in your Lodge.

❑ Attend on the Worshipful Master and Wardens, to act as their proxy in the active duties of the Lodge; such as the reception of candidates into the different degrees of Freemasonry, the introduction and accommodation of visiting brethren and visitors, and the immediate practice of our rites.

❑ Serve as Lodge Historian, if there is not one so appointed, and maintain a scrapbook binder of the events of the Lodge to be placed in the Archives of the Lodge for the year. Responsible for maintaining the Lodge Archives and memorabilia, as well as the Lodge Library.

❑ Maintain a binder of the published works of the Trestleboard, which will be placed and housed in the Lodge Library.

❑ Carry messages from the Senior Warden in the West to the Junior Warden in the South, and elsewhere about the Lodge as he may direct.

❑ Assist the Senior Deacon as needed or required, serving as his proxy in his absence.

❑ With the Senior Deacon, attend to the Lodge Room by ensuring the room is clean and prepared, Secretary's trash can is emptied, and aprons and jewels are laid out before and counted and properly stored after all meetings.

❏ _____

_____

_____

❏ _____

_____

_____

❏ _____

_____

_____

❏ _____

_____

_____

❏ _____

_____

_____

Degree Work

As Junior Deacon, you should learn the Junior Deacon's Opening and Closing parts for meetings, the Senior Deacon's Opening and Closing parts for meetings, and the Senior Deacon's part in the ritual work for all three degrees. You should attend as many degrees this year as you can.

Once you have mastered the Junior Deacon's parts, then you should begin learning the Senior Deacon's parts. If you have the time to learn it, you should then start working on learning the EA Charge and Apron Lecture. You should also attend your Lodge's Practice Night with the Senior Deacon, so that you can learn and improve on the floor work for the Deacon's parts in the degrees.

IF YOUR LODGE DOES NOT MEET FOR A REGULARLY SCHEDULED PRACTICE NIGHT, THEN SPEAK WITH YOUR MASTER AND WARDENS AND START ONE.

Junior Deacon Proficiency Checklist

Date Completed	Part Learned
	Junior Deacon, Meeting Opening
	Junior Deacon, Meeting Closing
	Senior Deacon, Meeting Opening
	Senior Deacon, Meeting Closing
	Senior Deacon, 1st Section – EA Degree
	Senior Deacon, 1st Section – FC Degree
	Senior Deacon, 1st Section – MM Degree
	Candidate Charge – EA Degree
	SW's Apron Lecture – EA Degree

Degree Work as Junior Deacon

Date	Degree	Part	Lodge
3-1-13	MM	JD	Masonic Lodge No 789 FAM

Personal Notes as Junior Deacon

Personal Notes as Junior Deacon

Personal Notes as Junior Deacon

_____

_____

_____

_____

_____

_____

_____

_____

_____

_____

_____

_____

_____

_____

_____

_____

_____

_____

_____

4 SENIOR DEACON

It is in this position that a man comes to learn about the inner workings of the Lodge and how 2 + 2 sometimes have to equal 3 or 5. No man should serve in the position of Warden until he has first served in the position of Senior Deacon. This point can in no way be stressed enough by any one in any Lodge. Advancing a man to the Office of Warden, who has not served as the Senior Deacon, is doing him an injustice and setting him up to fail.

His duty is as messenger of the Worshipful Master, hence he does a lot of walking. The Senior Deacon carries a blue Staff, topped with a sun emblem inside the Square and Compasses while at Labour in the Lodge.

The Jewel of his office is the Square and Compass with the Sun in the middle. The sun signifies that his position is on the lower level, to the right of the Worshipful Master in the east.

The Senior Deacon of a Masonic Lodge is an assistant officer of the Lodge. The Senior Deacon's principle roles are to welcome and escort both visitors and candidates into the lodge and introduce distinguished visitors.

It is his duty to assist the Worshipful Master and carry orders between the Worshipful Master and the Senior Warden. During degree rituals, he guides the new candidate and conducts him around the lodge room. He is the Worshipful Master's right hand in most things.

He is appointed by and can be removed at will by the Worshipful Master.

During the opening and closing ceremonies, the Senior Deacon opens the Volume of Sacred Law to the correct passage of the degree being worked and closes it after the lodge is adjourned. He also lights and extinguishes the Lesser Lights at the altar. He prepares, attends to, and carries the ballot box around the lodge when new members or candidates for office are being voted upon.

The Senior Deacon (and the Junior Deacon) both carry long staffs (or rods), because as messengers of the Worshipful Master, the staffs are symbolic of the caduceus (or wand) that the Roman winged god and messenger Mercury carried during their duties. Atop the rods are the jewels of their offices.

The Senior Deacon's position is similar to a Manager.

The following are the proposed duties of the Senior Deacon, but may be amended by your Lodge By-laws, situation at hand, and the order of the Worshipful Master or the Wardens in his stead:

Suggested Duties of the Senior Deacon

Check or fill in the Senior Deacon's Duties in your Lodge.

❑ Attend on the Worshipful Master and Wardens, to act as their proxy in the active duties of the Lodge; such as the reception of candidates into the different degrees of Freemasonry, the introduction and accommodation of visiting brethren and visitors, and the immediate practice of our rites.

❑ With the Secretary or his appointee, assist by witnessing the questions asked to and answers given by the Candidate for the Entered Apprentice Degree, as published in the Masonic Code of your jurisdiction, prior to the Candidate's first admission into the Lodge Room for the First Degree of Freemasonry.

❑ Assist the Marshal or Master of Ceremonies in his duties as needed or required.

❑ Examine and introduce all visiting Brethren. In the event that the visiting Brother is a stranger and hails from some Lodge in another Grand Jurisdiction, the Senior Deacon will assist the Secretary and Tyler in preparing the appropriate notification to be sent to the visitor's Lodge that we have had the pleasure of his visit.

❑ It shall be his (or his proxy's) duty to prepare, receive, and conduct all candidates in the various degrees.

❑ Organize and attend degree work training sessions under the direction of the Senior Warden.

❑ Serve as Committee Chairman for the Annual Senior Deacon's Work Project. If your Lodge does not have a Senior Deacon's Work Project, you should seek to establish one. It provides the Senior Deacon with his first opportunity to plan, organize and run a Lodge Event, giving him a view of what it takes to hold an event. It should be an event open to the public, which requires coordination with other organizations and community agencies, and may be charitable or social in nature.

❑ Serve as Degree Captain for all Entered Apprentice Degrees conducted by the Lodge; prepare the cast; notify the Candidate of the time and place for the degree.

❑ Carry orders from the Worshipful Master in the East to the Senior Warden in the West, and elsewhere about the Lodge as he may direct.

❏ Assist the Junior Deacon as needed or required, serving as his proxy in his absence.

❏ With the Junior Deacon, attend to the Lodge Room by ensuring the room is clean and prepared, trash can is emptied, and aprons and jewels are laid out before and counted and properly stored after all meetings.

❏ _____

_____

_____

❏ _____

_____

_____

❏ _____

_____

_____

❏ _____

_____

_____

Ideas for Your Senior Deacon's Work Project

These ideas are from the HANDBOOK ON LODGE COMMUNITY SERVICE PROJECTS with permission from the Most Worshipful Grand Lodge of the Commonwealth of Virginia, A.F.&A.M.:

GROUP A - Projects to Help Your Community

A-1 Organize the Brethren to Learn Cardio Pulmonary Resuscitation and First Aid

A-2 Have an Active Lodge Blood Donor/Pheresis Program

A-3 Support a Marrow Transplant Register and Organ Donor Awareness Program

A-4 Have the Lodge Involved in Community Disaster Preparedness Projects

A-5 Establish a Community Emergency Shelter at the Lodge

A-6 Organize or Participate in a Neighborhood Watch Program

A-7 Support a Battered Women's Shelter

A-8 Have the Lodge Partner with the Community to Provide Home Management Guidance

A-9 Provide Space at the Lodge for Job Fairs

A-10 Collect Books for the Local Library

A-11 Sponsor a Neighborhood Fair

A-12 Present Patriotic Programs in Various Public Settings, Including Flag Presentation

A-13 Conduct Child ID Programs at Schools, Community Events, Health Fairs, etc.

A-14 Sponsor or Coach a Little League Sports Team

A-15 Perform a Cemetery Survey

A-16 Organize a Group of Lodge Brethren to be Volunteer "Guides" at Historical Sites and Monuments and publicize these Sites and Monuments among high school and college students

A-17 Sponsor or assist a Local Historical Site or Museum

A-18 Have the Lodge Develop Maps or Other Walking or Driving Tours of Identified Historical Sites and Points of Interest, and Conduct Tours

A-19 Honor Community Volunteers and Professional Service Providers

GROUP B - Projects to Help the Environment

B-20 Plant a Tree
B-21 Adopt-A-Field
B-22 Adopt a Stream
B-23 Adopt a Wilderness Area or Cave
B-24 Adopt-A-Highway
B-25 Adopt a Cemetery
B-26 Start a Lodge Project to Encourage Recycling
B-27 Start a Lodge Project to Encourage Energy Savings

GROUP C - Projects to Assist Various Charities

C-28 Sponsor a Charity Walk-A-Thon
C-29 Sponsor a Charity Race or Marathon
C-30 Sponsor a Charity Bike-A-Thon
C-31 Answer Phones on Telethons and Radio-thons
C-32 Support to a Specific Charitable Organization

GROUP D - Projects to Assist the Aged

D-33 Set up a Program for Daily Phone Calls to the Elderly
D-34 Assist the Meals-on-Wheels Program
D-35 Regularly Visit and Assist Shut-ins
D-36 Assist a Pet's for Seniors Program
D-37 Provide Personalized Shopping Service for the Aged
D-38 Transportation Clearinghouse
D-39 Set up a Home Maintenance and Repair Program for the Aged
D-40 Nursing Home Visitation

GROUP E - Projects to Assist the Handicapped

E-41 Produce a Public Facility "Locator" for Handicapped Visitors
E-42 Participate in a Program to Read to and/or Record Books for the Blind
E-43 Sponsor a Picnic or Swim Party for Handicapped Children
E-44 Sponsor, Encourage or Coach a Special Olympian
E-45 Handicapped Citizen Family Services Program

GROUP F - Projects to Assist the Sick

F-46 Organize the Lodge to Participate in the Grant-A-Wish Program

F-47 Start or Participate in a Hospital Visitation Program

F-48 Provide Needed Services to the Family of a Hospitalized, Chronically Ill, or Dying Patient

GROUP G - Projects to Assist to Educate the Children and Others

G-49 Sponsor an Essay Contest, particularly on Patriotic Topic

G-50 Sponsor a Poster Project on a Patriotic, Substance Abuse, or Public Education Theme

G-51 Sponsor a Student Citizenship Award Program

G-52 Prepare Historical Reenactments for Schools

G-53 Recognize Educators at Teacher of the Year Programs

G-54 Provide Recycled Art/Handicraft Materials for Schools

G-55 Support Public Education

G-56 Participate in a Child Reading Tutor Program and Help Sponsor a Summer Reading Program

G-57 Set Up a Student Assistance Program

G-58 Tutor an Illiterate Adult or an Immigrant

GROUP H - Projects to Assist Those in Need

H-59 Develop an Emergency Referral Services Handbook and Provide Family Tragedy Assistance

H-60 Support Programs that Conduct Pre-School Eye Screening

H-61 Provide School Supplies for Needy Children

H-62 Set Up a Christmas in April Program

H-63 Collect and Distribute Holiday Food and Gift Baskets

H-64 Support an Established Soup Kitchen

H-65 Set up a Community Food Bank

GROUP I - Projects to Assist Armed Forces Personnel and Veterans

I-66 Set Up a Program or Join an Existing Program (MSA) to Visit a Veteran's Hospital

I-67 Write Letters to Service Personnel, Especially Masons and Members from the Local Community

I-68 Mail "Care Packages" to Service Members

I-69 Provide Assistance to the Wife and Family of Service Personnel, Especially Masons who are Deployed

GROUP J - Miscellaneous Projects

J-70 Join the War on Drugs

J-71 Paint a Church

J-72 Traveler's Way-stop

J-73 Masonic Anniversaries

J-74 Collect Eye Glasses for the Lions Club

J-75 Joint Brotherhood Nights with Other Fraternal Organizations

J-76 Community Health Fair

GROUP K - Projects to Assist the Community to Learn More about the Lodge and Freemasonry

K-77 Make Lodge Building and Facilities Available for Public and Community Functions

K-78 Get Permission to Have Cornerstone Laying Ceremony for a Public Building

K-79 Sponsor a Neighborhood Event, Such as a Halloween Party

K-80 Have Open Lodge Days for the Community to Visit the Lodge and Learn About Freemasonry and What Goes On in the Building

Degree Work

As Senior Deacon, you should learn the Senior Deacon's Opening and Closing parts for meetings, the Junior Warden's Opening and Closing parts for meetings, the Junior Warden's part in the ritual work for all three degrees. You should attend as many degrees this year as you can.

Once you have mastered the Senior Deacon's parts, then you should begin learning the Junior Warden's parts.

If you have the time to learn it, you should then start working on learning the FC Charge and Senior Warden's Apron Lecture.

You should also attend your Lodge's Practice Night with the Junior Deacon, so that you can learn and improve on the floor work for the Deacon's parts in the degrees.

IF YOUR LODGE DOES NOT MEET FOR A REGULARLY SCHEDULED PRACTICE NIGHT, THEN SPEAK WITH YOUR MASTER AND WARDENS AND START ONE.

Senior Deacon Proficiency Checklist

Date Completed	Part Learned
	Senior Deacon, Meeting Opening
	Senior Deacon, Meeting Closing
	Junior Warden, Meeting Opening
	Junior Warden, Meeting Closing
	Junior Warden, 1st Section – EA Degree
	Junior Warden, 1st Section – FC Degree
	Junior Warden, 1st Section – MM Degree
	Candidate Charge – FC Degree
	SW's Apron Lecture – FC Degree

Degree Work as Senior Deacon

Date	Degree	Part	Lodge
3-1-13	EA	SD	Masonic Lodge No 987 AFM

Degree Work as Senior Deacon

Date	Degree	Part	Lodge
3-1-13	EA	SD	Masonic Lodge No 987 AFM

A Mason who has the opportunity to visit in other lodges may well recall the words of the Great Light upon the Altar, no less true for him than they were spoken in olden times; "Let us go again and visit our Brethren in every city" (acts 15:36).

Brethren of that lodge which has the privilege of acting as host to him who comes to the Tyler's door a stranger and enters the Lodge as a Brother may rejoice in the words: "Let Brotherly Love continue. Be not forgetful to entertain strangers, for thereby some have entertained angels unaware." (Hebrews 14:1, 2.)

Visitors Welcomed & Accommodated as Senior Deacon

Date	Event	Name, Lodge and Lodge Address
3-1-13	EA	*John Smith* *Masonic Lodge No 987 AFM* *567 Lodge St, Anytown, ST 12345*

Visitors Welcomed & Accommodated as Senior Deacon

Date	Event	Name, Lodge and Lodge Address

Visitors Welcomed & Accommodated as Senior Deacon

Date	Event	Name, Lodge and Lodge Address

Visitors Welcomed & Accommodated as Senior Deacon

Date	Event	Name, Lodge and Lodge Address

Visitors Welcomed & Accommodated as Senior Deacon

Date	Event	Name, Lodge and Lodge Address

Visitors Welcomed & Accommodated as Senior Deacon

Date	Event	Name, Lodge and Lodge Address

Visitors Welcomed & Accommodated as Senior Deacon

Date	Event	Name, Lodge and Lodge Address

Visitors Welcomed & Accommodated as Senior Deacon

Date	Event	Name, Lodge and Lodge Address

Sample Letter to Visitor's Lodge

LODGE LETTERHEAD

___(Date)___

Masonic Lodge No. 123 AF&AM
123 Lodge St
Anytown, ST 12345

Dear Worshipful Master, Wardens & Brethren:

This letter is to notify you that we had the pleasure of
being visited by a Brother from your Lodge, Bro. _____, on
___(Date)___.

It was a pleasure to have him sit in our Lodge. We look forward to
seeing him again, as well as any other members of your Lodge.

Our Stated Meetings are held on the _____ of every month, and
we welcome you all to come and visit with us any time.

Should you need to contact us, please call ___(Phone)___ or email
us at __(email address)___.

In the Light,

(Signature)

Name
Worshipful Master
Your Lodge

Personal Notes as Senior Deacon

_____

_____

_____

_____

_____

_____

_____

_____

_____

_____

_____

_____

_____

_____

_____

_____

_____

_____

Personal Notes as Senior Deacon

_____

_____

_____

_____

_____

_____

_____

_____

_____

_____

_____

_____

_____

_____

_____

_____

_____

_____

Personal Notes as Senior Deacon

_____

_____

_____

_____

_____

_____

_____

_____

_____

_____

_____

_____

_____

_____

_____

_____

_____

Personal Notes as Senior Deacon

_____

_____

_____

_____

_____

_____

_____

_____

_____

_____

_____

_____

_____

_____

_____

_____

_____

5 THE JUNIOR WARDEN

The Junior Warden of a Masonic Lodge is the third in command of the Lodge. The Junior Warden sits in the South (symbolic of the position of the sun at midday) and is responsible for the Brethren while the Lodge is at ease or refreshment. His Jewel of Office is the Plumb,... which is a stonemason's instrument used for ascertaining the alignment of a vertical surface., and it symbolizes upright behavior among Masons. His position is similar to a Second Vice-President.

The Junior Warden, too, may open the lodge if the Master and Senior Warden are unable to attend the meeting.

He is elected by the members of his Lodge, and may only be removed from office under certain restrictions as listed in the Masonic Code of your jurisdiction.

It is the Junior Warden's duty to arrange meals for the lodge, and, typically, the two Stewards act as his assistants in this responsibility.

Symbolically, it is also his duty to make certain that the

members do not convert their refreshment into intemperance or excess. This is a holdover from earlier days, which still remains as part of the Junior Warden's job description, even though in most U.S. jurisdictions, alcohol is barred from the lodge.

The following are the proposed duties of the Junior Warden, but may be amended by your Lodge By-laws, situation at hand, and the order of the Worshipful Master or the Senior Warden in his stead:

Suggested Duties of the Junior Warden

Check or fill in the Junior Warden's Duties in your Lodge.

❑ When both Worshipful Master & Senior Warden are absent and cannot be reached with reasonable efforts, shall succeed to the duties of Worshipful Master, except in open Lodge, whereby the oldest Past Master present shall succeed to the duties of the Worshipful Master for the conduct of the meeting.

❑ Superintendence of the Craft during hours of refreshment.

❑ Serves as Ex-Officio Member on all Standing Committees.

❑ Prefer charges against offending Brethren and prosecute the same.

❑ Present charges in the manner required by the Masonic Code.

❑ Read selections from the Masonic Code at each Stated Meeting.

❑ Attend Grand Lodge communications.

❑ Direct the operations of the Stewards and Kitchen Manager.

❑ Oversees all operations at Labour, and recommends candidates to the Worshipful Master for committee chairmen for special "at Labour" projects, including, but not limited to:

- Family & Awards Night Banquets
- Fundraiser Dinners
- Annual Masonic Widows' Luncheons/Picnics
- Annual Past Masters' Table Lodges/Dinners
- Installation of Officers Receptions

❑ Serve as Degree Captain for all Fellow Craft Degrees conducted by the Lodge; prepare the cast; notify the Candidate of the time and place for the degree.

The Office of the Wardens (2 Years)

Leadership means many things to many people, but there is one constant in all forms of leadership. It is the ability to successfully manage others. Before one can effective lead, one must effectively manage the entity they are leading and the people that work within that entity.

As Junior Warden, you have the unique perspective of the Lodge. You are now off the floor and are able to see more of the workings of the Lodge.

Your time as Junior Warden should be used to note the activities and actions that work and those that need improvement. Try to understand the dynamics of the Lodge and the various roles that the members, officers and Past Masters play in the Lodge. It is also time to start thinking about the activities that you would like to have take place when you are in the East.

IF YOU ARE WORRIED ABOUT YOUR ABILITY TO SUCCESSFULLY MANAGE AND LEAD, DO NOT.

Your Brothers, and especially the Past Masters of your Lodge WILL NOT let you fail if you honestly try. This year, you are, for the first time, one of the three Senior Officers of your Lodge, and are responsible, in part, for its successful management.

OFFICERS of your year as JUNIOR WARDEN

Year _____

Office	Member	Phone
Worshipful Master	_____	_____
Junior Warden	_____	_____
Senior Warden	_____	_____
Treasurer	_____	_____
Secretary	_____	_____
Chaplain	_____	_____
Senior Deacon	_____	_____
Junior Deacon	_____	_____
Senior Steward	_____	_____
Junior Steward	_____	_____
Tyler	_____	_____
Marshal	_____	_____
Master Educator	_____	_____
Master of Ceremonies	_____	_____
Master of the Work (Ritual)	_____	_____
Lodge Trustee	_____	_____
Lodge Trustee	_____	_____
Lodge Trustee	_____	_____
Lodge Trustee	_____	_____
Lodge Trustee	_____	_____

Degree Work

As Junior Warden, you should learn the Junior Warden's Opening and Closing parts for meetings, the Senior Warden's Opening and Closing parts for meetings, the Senior Warden's part in the ritual work for all three degrees. You should attend as many degrees this year as you can.

Once you have mastered the Junior Warden's parts, then you should begin learning the Senior Warden's parts.

If you have the time to learn it, you should then start working on learning the MM Charge and Senior Warden's Apron Lecture.

You should also attend your Lodge's Practice Night with the Senior Warden, so that you can learn and improve on the floor work for the Warden's parts in the degrees.

IF YOUR LODGE DOES NOT MEET FOR A REGULARLY SCHEDULED PRACTICE NIGHT, THEN SPEAK WITH YOUR MASTER AND SENIOR WARDEN AND START ONE.

Junior Warden's Proficiency Checklist

Date Completed	Part Learned
	Junior Warden, Meeting Opening
	Junior Warden, Meeting Closing
	Senior Warden, Meeting Opening
	Senior Warden, Meeting Closing
	Senior Warden, 1st Section – EA Degree
	Senior Warden, 1st Section – FC Degree
	Senior Warden, 1st Section – MM Degree
	Candidate Charge – MM Degree
	SW's Apron Lecture – MM Degree
	Rules of Order in Lodge
	Familiarization with your Masonic Code Book
	Familiarization with the Junior Warden's Responsibilities within your Masonic Code

Degree Work as Junior Warden

Date	Degree	Part	Lodge
3-1-13	FC	JW	Masonic Lodge No 654 F&AM-PHA

Degree Work as Junior Warden

Date	Degree	Part	Lodge

Degree Work as Junior Warden

Date	Degree	Part	Lodge

Stated Meeting Code Readings as Junior Warden

Code Number	Topic

Personal Notes as Junior Warden

_____

_____

_____

_____

_____

_____

_____

_____

_____

_____

_____

_____

_____

_____

_____

_____

Personal Notes as Junior Warden

_____

_____

_____

_____

_____

_____

_____

_____

_____

_____

_____

_____

_____

_____

_____

_____

_____

_____

Personal Notes as Junior Warden

Personal Notes as Junior Warden

Personal Notes as Junior Warden

6 THE SENIOR WARDEN

The Senior Warden of a Masonic Lodge is the second in command within the Lodge Officers, and his Jewel is the Level...symbolizing that all Masons meet on the level, without regard to social, political or religious beliefs or status. His office is equivalent to a Vice-President in any organization.

His ancient duties were to pay the Craft (the members of the guild) their wages and to handle disputes among the workers. It is his duty to support the Master and to prepare himself for that office during the following year.

In the absence of the Worshipful Master, the Senior Warden assumes the Worshipful Master's duties. The Senior Warden of a Masonic Lodge sits in the West (symbolic of the setting sun) and assists the Worshipful Master in opening and closing the Lodge.

He is elected by the members of his Lodge and may only be removed under certain conditions as specified in the Masonic Code of your jurisdiction.

The Senior Warden is in charge of the Lodge when it is at labor.

The following are the proposed duties of the Senior Warden, but may be amended by your Lodge By-laws, situation at hand, and the order of the Worshipful Master or the appointed Past Master in his stead:

Suggested Duties of the Senior Warden

Check or fill in the Senior Warden's Duties in your Lodge.

❑ Succeeds to all duties of the Worshipful Master when the Worshipful Master is absent.

❑ In the absence of the Worshipful Master to govern the Lodge; in his presence, to assist him.

❑ Serves as Ex-Officio Member on all Standing Committees.

❑ Attends Grand Lodge Communications.

❑ Oversees all operations at Labour, and recommends candidates to the Worshipful Master for committee chairmen for special "at Labour" projects, including, but not limited to:

- o Grand Lodge Quarry Meetings – when the Lodge hosts the meeting.
- o Grand Lecturer's Schools of Instruction – when the Lodge hosts the school.
- o Lodge Practice Sessions
- o Community Service Projects
- o Community Events Participation
- o Joint Masonic Events
- o Joint Lodge-Other Non-Masonic Organization Events
- o Degree Work
- o Installation of Officers Ceremony

❑ Serve as Degree Captain for all Master Mason Degrees conducted by the Lodge; prepare the cast; notify the Candidate of the time and place for the degree.

❏ _____

_____

_____

❏ _____

_____

_____

❏ _____

_____

_____

❏ _____

_____

_____

❏ _____

_____

_____

Your Year as Senior Warden

This monthly checklist is suggested by our Brothers in the Grand Lodge of Minnesota, A.F.&A.M., and has been cited and adapted for use here with permission from their Lodge Leadership Notebook (2008):

First Month (as Senior Warden)

It is never too soon to begin preparation for your year as Master. You should be getting to know the brethren in the Lodge. You should be thinking about the members in the appointed offices, as well as determining the ability and interest of the membership. You should also be active in local Lodge Associations and getting to know your District Representative and other Grand Lodge Officers.

Remember, "politics" is only a bad word if you make it so. Political activity is not allowed in our Lodges; but interaction with other Lodges, Grand Lodge officers and other "movers and shakers" is a necessary ingredient in your success as a Lodge leader. Ensure you participate in regular officer's meetings, so that you learn the ropes early.

A regular theme for this program will be to consider how you would change things, or do things differently during your year. We want you to build upon the past, both from the successes and from the occasional mistake.

Second Month

You should be considering a rough outline of what you want to do during the following year. For example, try envisioning your installation ceremony. You should have attended a couple of these by now, so you should know the general program.

Think about who will most likely be in those positions of support. Who will be the team supporting you next year? Each Lodge has to adjust and it's easier to do so in advance than at the last minute.

Third Month

Review the calendar for the current year. What is working? What should be changed? With this in mind, begin to plan your calendar for next year. Familiarize yourself with:

(1) Your Lodge publication(s)
(2) Other Lodge publications
(3) Minutes of Lodge meetings
(4) The Lodge finances
(5) Where money goes
(6) Where money comes from

You should be familiarizing yourself with how a Lodge is governed. Also, how does your Lodge differ in its governance from other Lodges? An experienced Past Master or your District Representative will know.

Fourth Month

Establish a good "counseling" relationship with the Past Masters. They should be your best resource. They will be your best resource if you reach out to them and involve them in your decision making process. Don't just ask them to tell you what you should be doing. Instead, ask for and listen to their input for when you make the decision.

Fifth Month

Continue to plan, PLAN, PLAN! Begin to put actual dates to events. Familiarize yourself with the calendars of all appendant bodies that might affect or conflict with your schedule for the following year. Go ahead and put those events on the calendar contained in this notebook.

Then you can plan your year around them. Maintain an open dialog with the current Master so you stay "in the loop" on all of the problems and pitfalls that he is encountering as he progresses through his year. You also should know if the current officers want to move up to the next chair. You should now know which men you want to appoint to office.

Sixth, Seventh & Eighth Months

This is the time that you should be reviewing the successes and failures of the current year with the sitting Master. These summer months are wonderful opportunities for you to learn about the Lodge, its history, its finances and its quirks. These months also provide opportunities for morning coffee with a possible officer or lunch with a possible committee chairman.

Take the Master out to dinner and discuss with him your plans. He will have valuable insights for you that only experience can bring. This is the time to share your vision and plans and, thereby, set up support for those visions and plans.

Ninth Month

By the end of the ninth month you, should have confirmed with all line officers their desire and commitment to move up to the next chair. You should also make tentative appointment of any new officer, pending your election. With the approval and involvement of the current Master, you should have your first officer's meeting.

Certainly a great assumption is being made here, since there is always the possibility that you, the Senior Warden or the Junior Warden, will not be elected to your aspired offices. However, that being said, it is reasonable and proper for you to begin plans for all activities for the coming year.

Committees should be provisionally appointed and their planning should begin, with periodic progress reports being made to you. In particular, you should keep in touch with your Master Educator to discuss the content and tone of possible educational programs for the Lodge.

Tenth & Eleventh Months

Continue to plan and implement. This is critical time, but if you spend it productively you can have everything in place and ready to go by the middle of the eleventh month. By this point your Master Educator should have a schedule of speakers for at least the first half of the coming year, and you should finalize plans for election night and for your installation.

Twelfth Month

Relax! Enjoy the holidays, for you are going to be quite busy for the next twelve months!

Paying Wages to the Craft, if any Be Due Them

As Bro. Benjamin Franklin so eloquently stated over two centuries ago:

"If a man empties his purse into his head, no man can take it away from hi. An investment in knowledge always pays the best interest. Masonic labor is purely a labor of love. He who seeks to draw Masonic wages in silver and gold will be disappointed. The wages of a Mason are earned and paid in their dealings with one another; sympathy that begets sympathy, kindness begets kindness, helpfulness begets helpfulness, and these are the wages of a Mason."

Whenever a Mason does Masonic good, whether that be physical or mental assistance with helping further Masonic ideals, ideas, projects, events, activities, or anything else, DO NOT fail to pay him his wages among the Craft. As Senior Warden, it is your sworn duty to do so.

All Freemasons are entitled to receive their wages, and if they do not, it is owing to the wilful neglect of their duties; it is their fault, and not the fault of the craft.

USE THE FOLLOWING RECORD SHEETS TO KEEP TRACK OF WORK PERFORMED BY ACTIVE MASONS, SO YOU CAN RECOGNIZE THEM IN YOUR MONTHLY STATED MEETINGS AS

RECIPIENTS OF MASTER'S WAGES IN THE QUARRIES:

SENIOR WARDEN'S MONTHLY PAY RECORD
FOR MASTER'S WAGES for MONTH _____

Name(s)_____

Event_____ Date_____

Work Performed_____

_____

_____

Name(s)_____

Event_____ Date_____

Work Performed_____

_____

_____

Name(s)_____

Event_____ Date_____

Work Performed_____

_____

_____

SENIOR WARDEN'S MONTHLY PAY RECORD
FOR MASTER'S WAGES for MONTH _____

Name(s)_____

Event_____ Date_____

Work Performed_____

_____

_____

Name(s)_____

Event_____ Date_____

Work Performed_____

_____

_____

Name(s)_____

Event_____ Date_____

Work Performed_____

_____

_____

SENIOR WARDEN'S MONTHLY PAY RECORD
FOR MASTER'S WAGES for MONTH _____

Name(s)_____

Event_____ Date_____

Work Performed_____

_____

_____

Name(s)_____

Event_____ Date_____

Work Performed_____

_____

_____

Name(s)_____

Event_____ Date_____

Work Performed_____

_____

_____

SENIOR WARDEN'S MONTHLY PAY RECORD
FOR MASTER'S WAGES for MONTH _____

Name(s)_____

Event_____ Date_____

Work Performed_____

_____

_____

Name(s)_____

Event_____ Date_____

Work Performed_____

_____

_____

Name(s)_____

Event_____ Date_____

Work Performed_____

_____

_____

SENIOR WARDEN'S MONTHLY PAY RECORD
FOR MASTER'S WAGES for MONTH _____

Name(s)_____

Event_____ Date_____

Work Performed_____

_____

_____

Name(s)_____

Event_____ Date_____

Work Performed_____

_____

_____

Name(s)_____

Event_____ Date_____

Work Performed_____

_____

_____

SENIOR WARDEN'S MONTHLY PAY RECORD
FOR MASTER'S WAGES for MONTH _____

Name(s)_____

Event_____ Date_____

Work Performed_____

_____

_____

Name(s)_____

Event_____ Date_____

Work Performed_____

_____

_____

Name(s)_____

Event_____ Date_____

Work Performed_____

_____

_____

SENIOR WARDEN'S MONTHLY PAY RECORD
FOR MASTER'S WAGES for MONTH _____

Name(s)_____

Event_____ Date_____

Work Performed_____

_____

_____

Name(s)_____

Event_____ Date_____

Work Performed_____

_____

_____

Name(s)_____

Event_____ Date_____

Work Performed_____

_____

_____

SENIOR WARDEN'S MONTHLY PAY RECORD
FOR MASTER'S WAGES for MONTH _____

Name(s)_____

Event_____ Date_____

Work Performed_____

_____

_____

Name(s)_____

Event_____ Date_____

Work Performed_____

_____

_____

Name(s)_____

Event_____ Date_____

Work Performed_____

_____

_____

SENIOR WARDEN'S MONTHLY PAY RECORD
FOR MASTER'S WAGES for the MONTH _____

Name(s)_____

Event_____ Date_____

Work Performed_____

_____

_____

Name(s)_____

Event_____ Date_____

Work Performed_____

_____

_____

Name(s)_____

Event_____ Date_____

Work Performed_____

_____

_____

SENIOR WARDEN'S MONTHLY PAY RECORD
FOR MASTER'S WAGES for MONTH _____

Name(s)_____

Event_____ Date_____

Work Performed_____

_____

_____

Name(s)_____

Event_____ Date_____

Work Performed_____

_____

_____

Name(s)_____

Event_____ Date_____

Work Performed_____

_____

_____

SENIOR WARDEN'S MONTHLY PAY RECORD
FOR MASTER'S WAGES for MONTH _____

Name(s)_____

Event_____ Date_____

Work Performed_____

_____

_____

Name(s)_____

Event_____ Date_____

Work Performed_____

_____

_____

Name(s)_____

Event_____ Date_____

Work Performed_____

_____

_____

OFFICERS of your year as SENIOR WARDEN

Year _____

Office	Member	Phone
Worshipful Master	_____	_____
Junior Warden	_____	_____
Senior Warden	_____	_____
Treasurer	_____	_____
Secretary	_____	_____
Chaplain	_____	_____
Senior Deacon	_____	_____
Junior Deacon	_____	_____
Senior Steward	_____	_____
Junior Steward	_____	_____
Tyler	_____	_____
Marshal	_____	_____
Master Educator	_____	_____
Master of Ceremonies	_____	_____
Master of the Work (Ritual)	_____	_____
Lodge Trustee	_____	_____
Lodge Trustee	_____	_____
Lodge Trustee	_____	_____
Lodge Trustee	_____	_____
Lodge Trustee	_____	_____
_____	_____	_____
_____	_____	_____
_____	_____	_____
_____	_____	_____
_____	_____	_____
_____	_____	_____
_____	_____	_____
_____	_____	_____
_____	_____	_____

Start Thinking About Member Assignments

Adapted with permission from the Grand Lodge of Virginia, A.F.&A.M., Publication: JOBS TO GIVE THE BRETHRN TO KEEP THEM ACTIVE AND ENGAGED AND KEEP THE LODGE HEALTHY AND PRODUCTIVE

Once you assume the Oriental Chair in the East, it will become your job to "set the Craft to Labour..."

In the Lodge, there is no such thing as a sideliner. There are only active and inactive Masons. To keep a Brother active you need to ensure that he has some responsibility in the Lodge: a job, a function, a role to play so that he feels he is a necessary part of the Lodge.

As the Worshipful Master, it is your responsibility to provide every Brother with a job in the Lodge. The old standby of asking every new Mason to be a Steward or to join the Line should be avoided. Not every Brother wants to be a Steward. Indeed, for some, this is totally unrelated to why they wanted to become a Mason and will be unwelcome. Similarly, many new Masons do not have the time to become an elected Lodge officer, and do not feel ready or qualified to accept this responsibility. But these new Brethren are enthusiastic and they want to get involved. The good news is that there is a job for every Mason, new or old that will be appealing, and will capitalize on his strengths and interests. Your challenge is to find a function that is appropriate for each Brother that is consistent with his interests, skills, and available time.

Giving each Brother a job is not only necessary for member retention; it is necessary to the health and strength of the Lodge, and to your success as Worshipful Master. What you will be able to accomplish for your Lodge and for Freemasonry will depend in no small part on the size of the pool of Brethren you can call upon. It is important

Set forth below are just a few of the categories of jobs you can give your members. Consider this list as a starting point, then think about the goals and objectives you have set, and what you hope to achieve during the year. Next seek out Brethren who can help you to reach these goals by taking on some of the responsibility.

I. Ritual

For a number of new Masons, the ritual is an important attraction. They love the ritual and want to see it performed. But they may not step forward and volunteer to participate, and they may not take the initiative to learn a part. They need to be asked. It is not sufficient to suggest that they take a part in one of the degrees. You need to be very specific. Tell him: "I need you to learn "x" part which has "y" lines, and I need you to be ready at "z" date." You should also explain to the Brother why it is important to the Lodge that he learns that particular part, for example, so the Lodge can perform a particular degree without outside help. Note, even if your Lodge does not have a candidate, it is still important to keep proficient in the ritual, and you should exemplify the degrees each year at a stated or called communication.

When you add together all of the parts in the three degrees, and the lectures, the charges, and the funeral service, there are forty-eight parts. Therefore, if you encourage your members to learn a specific part of our ritual you can have forty-eight Brethren actively engaged in activities needed by the Lodge. Some of these parts are short, others are more lengthy; some are totally unwritten, and others are mostly written. The point is that you can select a part that is within the capabilities of virtually every Brother.

II. Masonic Education

Many of the Brethren joined Freemasonry because they were interested in the Fraternity, its history and traditions, its philosophy and values. They want to know more about Masonic symbolism, famous Masons, and some of our charitable endeavors.

You can capitalize on this interest by approaching a number of the Brethren and asking them to prepare a brief paper on some aspect of Freemasonry to present at a stated communication. Remember not to neglect the inactive Brethren who may be waiting for an invitation to become more active. Tell them you only want a five-minute presentation and give them a set date when you want them to be on the program. If all you are asking for is a five-minute talk you can easily fit two such talks into your schedule at each stated communication. If you do this, you will be able to give twenty-four Brethren a useful function each year.

Some Brethren will be self-starters and able to come up with a virtually endless number of topics, others will have "writer's block" and need your help in generating ideas. You can help these Brethren by getting a supply of good books on Freemasonry and looking in the index or table of contents for topics to suggest. You can get additional topic ideas from the many "Short Talk" bulletins published by the Masonic Service Association, and from the many good Masonic websites.

The benefits of enlisting the Brethren to prepare these five-minute talks are many. First, the Brother preparing the talk will learn more about Freemasonry by reading the book or chapter you may have pointed out, by finding other books, or by doing research on the Internet. Second, his efforts will improve your meetings. Third, there is a benefit for all the Brethren. They will leave each meeting knowing more about Freemasonry than when they arrived, and they will be more motivated to attend the next meeting.

If you integrate this idea into your advance planning, you can tell all twenty-four Brethren about the full set of topics, and when each Brother is scheduled to speak on each topic. You may be able to generate enough interest that many of the speakers will decide to attend all of the meetings to hear the short talks the other Brethren will be presenting.

Masonic education can provide additional avenues for greater involvement by your members.

Here are a few additional ideas that can occupy thirty more of the Brethren.

• Appoint an Lodge Education Officer (Master Educator).
• Appoint three Brothers to give a short talk during the break in each of our three degrees.
• Appoint a Brother to read a section from the Book of Constitutions at each stated communication.
• Appoint a knowledgeable Brother to start a Masonic study group.
• Appoint twelve Brothers and ask each of them to go through ten of the questions and answers (Q & As) from the candidate alternate method EA/FC/MM degree booklets at a stated communication. Over the course of the year, you will have covered one hundred twenty questions, a little more than half of the Q & As in the three booklets. In less than two years, you can cover the entire set of Q & As.
• Appoint twelve Brothers to be responsible for one longer talk at Lodge — or for reading the monthly talk provided by the Grand Lodge Committee on Masonic Education.

When you add together all of these opportunities to participate in the educational program in your Lodge, you can have forty-eight

Brethren actively engaged on tasks that will help to make your Lodge meetings more interesting and exciting.

III. Communication

There was a time when everyone in America knew quite a lot about Freemasonry, understood our values, and looked with great favor on our many charitable endeavors. Today, fewer Americans know much about us, and we need to re-educate them about who we are and what we do. A Grand Lodge Public Relations Committee has been formed to address this issue, but there is much that each Lodge can do to enhance its reputation in the community and improve public perception of Freemasonry. To accomplish this important task, you need to delegate responsibility to a number of the Brethren to develop and implement an effective external communications program. This allows you to offer important jobs to qualified Brethren. Here are some ideas for your consideration:

• Appoint a Brother to develop an external communications plan to present to a Lodge officer's meeting or to the Lodge.

• Appoint a Brother to write press releases to be sent to the local newspapers and 20-, 30-, and 60-second public service radio spots to publicize Lodge projects such as Child ID or blood drives.

• Appoint a Brother to run a "Bring a Friend Night."

• Appoint a Brother to select a candidate for the annual Community Builders Award.

• Appoint a Brother to maintain contact with the Boy and Girl Scouts to set up the Lodge presentation of the Grand Lodge Certificate for Eagle Scouts and Girl Scout Gold Award winners.

• Appoint a Brother to take pictures at Lodge events and write a paragraph to send to the Masonic Herald.

• Appoint a Brother to maintain and develop the Lodge website.

An internal communications program is no less important to the health of the Lodge. It is important that you inform the Brethren of Lodge events well in advance so they can put them on the calendar. It is important that you stay in touch with all of the Brethren on a regular basis. You need to strengthen the bonds with the Brethren, and they need to know that their Lodge cares about them. It is important that you maintain regular contact with the widows to determine if they are well or if they need help from the Lodge.

Implementing an effective internal communications program will also allow you to offer important jobs to qualified Brethren. Here are some more ideas for your consideration.

• Appoint a couple of Brothers to help write the monthly Trestleboard.

• Appoint ten active Brethren to form a Lodge telephone committee. They would be asked to call one of the ten Brothers on their list each night, speaking for no more than five minutes, asking after his health and his family, and updating him on Lodge activities. Expending only five minutes a day, a telephone committee member will be able to speak with each Brother on his list once every two weeks (ten days), and your ten active members will be able to stay in regular contact with one hundred of the Brethren.

• Appoint a Brother to set up a widows committee made up of older Brethren who may not get to Lodge, and have each of them call one or two of the widows each day to check that they are all right. They would report back to the Lodge when there is a problem, and provide a general report on the widows before each stated communication.

• Appoint a Brother to be liaison to each of the youth groups sponsored by the Lodge, have him attend at least two of their meetings each year, and be responsible for having them come to Lodge once each year to put on a program.

• Appoint a Brother to be liaison to each of the other

organizations meeting at the Lodge: the Order of the Eastern Star, the Royal Arch, etc.

• One additional idea is to appoint a Brother at the beginning of your year to be your historian. Ask him to keep a record of the accomplishments and other highlights of the Masonic year, put it in narrative form, and present it to you and the Lodge at the end of the year. If the Lodge will do this every year, it will be very easy to write an interesting history of your Lodge.

When you add together all of these opportunities to participate in the internal and external communications program that is so important to the Lodge, you can have upwards of twenty-three tasks that you can offer to the Brethren.

IV. Lodge Administration and Maintenance

Keeping the Lodge open and working requires the cooperation of a number of Brethren. In addition, a good deal of effort is required to keep the Lodge building presentable so it makes a good impression in the community, is attractive to visitors and guests, and is an inviting place for the Brethren to attend. Here again are many responsibilities you give to your members that are important to the well-being of the Lodge.

Lodge Administration

• Appoint a Brother to head a committee or be a committee member.

• Appoint twelve Brethren, each of whom is to be responsible for helping you plan a meeting.

• Appoint a Brother to assist the Stewards in preparing the candidate and reading to the candidate the questions and answers in the Grand Lodge publication titled, Questions and Answers for the Postulant.

• Appoint a Brother to assist the Deacons in preparing the Lodge before the meeting and putting the regalia away at the end of the meeting.

• Appoint a Brother to take charge of washing the aprons and candidate clothing and keeping the Lodge equipment in good repair.

• Appoint Brethren to serve as one of the appointed officers.

• Appoint a Brother to be the Assistant Secretary and one to be the Assistant Treasurer. These appointments not only help the Secretary and Treasurer, they also help the Brethren appointed to better understand the operation of the Lodge.

• Appoint one or more of the Brethren to drive older members to and from the Lodge, so those who can't drive at night can attend.

• Appoint one or more of the Brethren to drive older members or widows to Lodge picnics, medical appointments, etc.

Lodge Maintenance

• Appoint a Brother to do an annual survey of the Lodge systems: heating and air conditioning, the roof, the gutters, the lights, windows and doors, etc., and report back to the Lodge.

• Appoint a Brother to come up with an annual prioritized improvement plan for the Lodge, i.e., painting, cleaning, redoing upholstery, and maintaining the altar and its furniture.

• Appoint a Brother to be in charge of each Lodge improvement project.

• Appoint a Brother to cut the grass.

• Appoint a Brother to be in charge of snow removal.

• Appoint a Brother to review the landscaping and suggest improvements.

V. Lodge Projects and Fundraisers

Second only to good programs at stated communications is a set of Lodge projects for keeping the Brethren active and engaged. When a spouse or colleague asks what your Lodge is doing, and the Brother can talk about a Lodge project that he is enthusiastic about, it shows Freemasonry in a very positive light, and it generates enthusiasm for others to join. In addition, because Lodges dues and investments often do not cover expenses, fund raising activities are necessary to cover the shortfall. Fund raising is also a way of generating money for our charities.

Each year the Worshipful Master should survey the Brethren for suggestions about projects that will enable the Lodge to contribute to the betterment of the community in which it is located. From this list, the Brethren should be asked to select the two or three projects they are most interested in doing, and these should be the projects you undertake. (You can find ideas about projects as well as suggestions about how to run them in the Grand Lodge publication, "100 Projects for Lodges to Consider.")

In the same way, the Worshipful Master should ask the Brethren to select from the myriad of fund raising ideas those that they want to support. There are only a few fund raising ideas, like gambling, that are not permitted. Virtually everything else from selling Christmas trees or sponsoring golf or tennis tournaments, to having a "yard sale" or a Lodge breakfast, lunch, or dinner that is open to the public is appropriate. (You can find more ideas about fund raising projects as well as suggestions about how to run them in the Grand Lodge publication, "100 Fund Raising Projects for Lodges to Consider.")

Each project allows you to offer some of the Brethren leadership opportunities and important roles to play.

• Appoint a Brother to be in charge of each project you select.

• Appoint both new and experienced Brethren to a committee that will plan each project, and engage the general Lodge membership in supporting it.

When you consider the ritual, educational, and communications programs, the Lodge administration and maintenance responsibilities, and the Lodge projects and fund raisers, you have over 150 separate opportunities to involve the Brethren in meaningful and important work in the Lodge – beyond serving as a Steward or becoming an elected Lodge officer.

Most Lodges will not have 150 Brethren without jobs, but this list, which is by no means complete, should convince you that there is a job for every Mason, new or old that will be appealing, and will capitalize on his strengths and interests.

It is essential that as Worshipful Master you ensure that every Brother have a job and a role to play in the Lodge.

Remember this is necessary for member retention, necessary to the health and strength of the Lodge, and important to your success as Worshipful Master.

Degree Work

As Senior Warden, you should learn the Senior Warden's Opening and Closing parts for meetings, the Worshipful Master's Opening and Closing parts for meetings, the Worshipful Master's part in the ritual work for all three degrees. You should attend as many degrees this year as you can.

Once you have mastered the Senior Warden's parts, then you should begin learning the Worshipful Master's parts.

You should also attend your Lodge's Practice Night with the Junior Warden, so that you can learn and improve on the floor work for the Warden's parts in the degrees.

IF YOUR LODGE DOES NOT MEET FOR A REGULARLY SCHEDULED PRACTICE NIGHT, THEN SPEAK WITH YOUR WORSHIPFUL MASTER AND START ONE.

Senior Warden's Proficiency Checklist

Date Completed	Part Learned
	Senior Warden, Meeting Opening
	Senior Warden, Meeting Closing
	Worshipful Master, Meeting Opening
	Worshipful Master, Meeting Closing
	Worshipful Master, 1st Section – EA Degree
	Worshipful Master, 1st Section – FC Degree
	Worshipful Master, 1st Section – MM Degree
	Worshipful Master – Rules of Order in Lodge
	Proficiency in using your Masonic Code Book

Degree Work as Senior Warden

Date	Degree	Part	Lodge
3-1-13	MM	SW	Masonic Lodge No 123 F&AM

Degree Work as Senior Warden

Date	Degree	Part	Lodge
3-1-13	MM	SW	Masonic Lodge No 123 F&AM

Candidate Tracking as Senior Warden

Candidate Name	Phone Number	EA Date	FC Date	MM Date
John Smith	555-555-5555	3-15-13	3-15-13	3-15-13

Candidate Tracking as Senior Warden

Candidate Name	Phone Number	EA Date	FC Date	MM Date
John Smith	555-555-5555	3-15-13	3-15-13	3-15-13

Personal Notes as Senior Warden

Personal Notes as Senior Warden

_____

_____

_____

_____

_____

_____

_____

_____

_____

_____

_____

_____

_____

_____

_____

_____

_____

_____

Personal Notes as Senior Warden

Personal Notes as Senior Warden

7 WORSHIPFUL MASTER

The Worshipful Master of a Masonic Lodge is the senior ranking officer of all Lodge Officers which a Lodge may elect. His Jewel is the Square, which is a stonemason's tool to ascertain true and correct angles of the cut and smoothed stone...thus his Jewel symbolizes virtue.

He is ultimately responsible for every other lodge officer and their duties, every lodge committee, ritual and degree work, Masonic education, social functions, fundraisers, District and Grand Lodge liaison, Trestle Board communication, etc.

HIS PRIMARY DUTY IS TO PROTECT THE CHARTER OF THE LODGE AND SEE THAT NO ACTION OR OFFENSE OCCURS DURING HIS TERM THAT WOULD JEOPARDIZE THE LOSING OF CHARTER.

The Worshipful Master sits in the East of the Lodge room (symbolic of the Rising Sun in the East) and directs all of the business of the Lodge. Note: Even if the building faces a different direction, the Master is said to be "in the East". He also presides over ritual and ceremonies. His position is equivalent to a President of any other organization. As Master, his word is final over any and all actions pertaining to his Lodge, and his decision is not subject to appeal.

It is his duty to: "Set the Craft to Labour, give them good and wholesome instruction or cause the same to be done".

While the Worshipful Master's rank is highest of all members, his Lodge Officer Duties are the easiest to remember. The Worshipful Master is responsible for every single thing within his lodge during his year as Master.

All eyes are upon the Master. If lodge functions go smoothly, it is the Master who takes the credit. If lodge functions go awry, it is the Master who bears the blame. Therefore, the Master wears many hats. It is his duty to preside over business meetings, the conferral of degrees, and delegation of duties to all other Lodge Officers.

While Freemasons call the Master, "Worshipful Master", they do not, as some people may erroneously believe, actually worship him. "Worshipful" is an honorary title which shows respect for his position. In France, the word "Worshipful" is replaced with the word "Venerable". It is no different than respecting the office of our President of the United States. He would be addressed, formally, as "Mr. President" rather than by his first name. Likewise, if you go before a judge, you would address him as "Your Honor", rather than by his first name, as a measure of respect that you hold for his office.

Suggested Duties of the Worshipful Master

Check or fill in the Worshipful Master's Duties in your Lodge.

❏ Protects the Charter of the Lodge.

❏ Attends Grand Lodge communications.

❏ Knows, understands and searches the Masonic Code at all times. Causes it to be read in the Lodge.

❑ Sees that the Code is adhered to in all Lodge operations and functions. Keeps a copy in the East at all meetings.

❑ Familiar with the Lodge By-Laws. Keeps a copy in the East at all meetings.

❑ Sees that the By-Laws of the Lodge and the Constitution and Regulations of the Grand Lodge are duly observed, and that the officers attend strictly to their duties.

❑ Serves as Ex-Officio Member on all Standing Committees.

❑ Fill vacancies pro tempore.

❑ Attends Stated and Called Meetings of appendant and concordant bodies that meet in his Lodge, or sends his representative to collect and report on the conduct of the meetings.

❑ Should not serve as an officer in any other appendant or concordant body that meets in his Lodge during his term of office to prevent conflict.

❑ Hold, or cause to be held, a regular monthly Officers Meeting of the Lodge Officers.

❑ Require audits.

❑ Attend as many Stated Meetings, Degrees, and Official Visits of other Lodges in the County and/or District as possible during the year.

Other assigned duties:

❑ _____

_____

_____

❏ _____

_____

_____

❏ _____

_____

_____

❏ _____

_____

_____

❏ _____

_____

_____

❏ _____

_____

_____

❏ _____

_____

_____

Your Year as Worshipful Master

This chapter has, in part, been adapted and expanded for use with permission of the Grand Lodge of Minnesota, A.F.&A.M., from their Lodge Leadership Notebook (2008):

You or your Lodge should develop a Lodge Leadership Notebook or Binder, containing the following tabs and information:

TAB 1: AGENDAS

Regular Meeting Agendas

Your agenda sets the tone for your meeting and helps you control the direction and duration of the meeting. It should be set up in advance for each meeting. It should be customized to fit your leadership style and the needs of your particular Lodge. Whether you wish to follow the structure that has been used in the past is a matter to be decided by you, as Master. It is important to set an agenda, so you can make sure that all of the things you want to accomplish in the meeting actually happen. It will also help you to stay on track through interruptions and keep the meeting moving along. You may, at your discretion, direct the Secretary to create this agenda. However, it is your responsibility to ensure one is made. The attached form is merely a sample, which could be copied and used as is or revised to fit your particular needs. Usually there are three main parts to a meeting; the opening, Lodge business, and a closing. There are many other things you could include, such as:

(1) Recognition of Past Masters
(2) Introduction of visitors
(3) Voting on business matters
(4) Presentations
(5) Lectures or educational programs
(6) Committee reports
(7) Officer reports
(8) Announcements (re: your Lodge and other Masonic bodies)
(9) Masonic education or program

(10) Lodge of Sorrow and the appropriate moment of silence

What you choose is up to you. You will be in charge, and your Lodge will be looking to you for leadership.

You may want to print a full or partial outline of the meeting for the members of your Lodge. Also, consider letting your officers and others know before the meeting what you will be doing, especially if they will be required to make a report to the Lodge.

While Masonic education or a program is listed late on the agenda, you need to budget time during the meeting so that you do have sufficient time for your speaker to make his presentation. You may want to move the presentation around from meeting to meeting, just to keep your members on their toes.

Officer's Meeting Agenda

An officer's meeting should be held at least once prior to your installation, to make sure all officers are informed of your plan. A good informed relationship with your officers will avoid problems and will enhance brotherhood within your Lodge. Another such meeting should be held after installation (but prior to the first stated meeting) to review your plan and make adjustments for any changes or additions. At this meeting you should specifically outline for your officers what your expectations are and make sure they are willing to work with you.

Some Lodges also hold these meetings monthly or quarterly to review the ongoing business of the Lodge. Included is a form that you may copy or revise and use to plan your officer's meetings. As with the regular meeting agenda form, you should adjust the form to fit your particular needs.

OFFICER'S MEETING AGENDA

Introduction
Old Business issues
New Business issues

Event/Activity assignments & expectations
Committee recommendations
Pending issues
Review of calendar

SAMPLE REGULAR MEETING AGENDA

Opening
Open on 3rd Degree
Lodge Business
Greetings and announcements by the Master
Introductions of visiting brothers by the Senior Deacon
Secretary's Report
Treasurer's Report
Junior Warden's Code Reading
Senior Warden's Report & Master's Wages
Committee Reports
Petitions – read / ballot
Old Business
New Business
Resolutions
Communications
Grand Lodge update by District Deputy
Appendant and Concordant Bodies updates
Announcement of upcoming Labor events by the Senior Warden
Announcement of upcoming Refreshment events by the Junior Warden
Announcements by visitors and members
Program of Masonic Instruction by the Master Educator
Passing of the Lectures – (If no lectures already passed during the Month per Code)
  • EA (JAN-APR-JUL-OCT);
  • FC (FEB-MAY-AUG-NOV);
  • MM (MAR-JUN-SEP-DEC)
Any other business as may lawfully come before the Lodge.
Closing
Master's closing remarks
Close on 3rd Degree

☐
☐
TAB 2: LODGE MINUTES

This is, of course, where you would place the minutes of the previous meetings. This can be useful to you when you are planning your next meeting or event, and you cannot recall what happened in a prior meeting. The secretary usually prepares the minutes. They may be passed out to the members in written form as the members enter the Lodge. The important thing is that the members know what is going on in the Lodge.

By avoiding a focus on record keeping in your Lodge meetings, the meetings will move along more smoothly and will be more interesting to the members. More than one Mason has reported that this section of the meeting, along with the Treasurer's report, is the most tedious. In view of that, a Master would be well advised to deal with these parts of the meeting with dispatch.

☐
TAB 3: LODGE FINANCES

One of your primary responsibilities as Master of your Lodge will be to manage the money. This is the section in which you would place the financial information about the Lodge that will guide you as Master. In this section, place copies of budgets and Treasurer's reports for the past couple of years to use as guidelines, together with your Lodge's current budget. The budget serves three basic functions.

First, the budget should provide you, your officers and the Lodge a quick explanation of how you are expecting to pay for the activities of the Lodge. Second, the budget should function as a short summary of the activities for the year. For example, a line item for a particular event will be a financial guideline for the person you place in charge of that event. Third, the budget gives you authority, as it has to be approved by the members of the Lodge, which in turn authorizes you to spend Lodge funds.

Included is an example form for making a budget. The sooner

you get started on this, the better. Because each Lodge varies in its activities and its finances, you will have to create a budget to meet your Lodge's specific needs. Using figures from previous years, you should be able to project where the income for the year will come from and how much it will cost to keep the Lodge running. Usually, the Secretary, the sitting Master and the Treasurer are the best people to confer with about the budget. Others to consult include prospective chairmen of your committees, fundraising committees, building officers, etc.

Your budget should be approved at your first stated meeting as Master of the Lodge. By doing so, you will be sending a clear message to the Lodge about what you have in mind for the New Year.

In some Lodges, the Senior Warden will present a budget for approval at the Annual Meeting of the Lodge, which approves the Treasurer's report of the previous year. Consult with Past Masters and your by-laws for direction on procedures applicable to your particular Lodge.

Sample Budget Worksheet

YOUR LODGE BUDGET	Q1	Q2	Q3	Q4
Expenses				
Rent/Taxes	_____	_____	_____	_____
Treasurer	_____	_____	_____	_____
Contributions	_____	_____	_____	_____
Physical Improvements	_____	_____	_____	_____
Other	_____	_____	_____	_____
Dues (less Per Diem)	_____	_____	_____	_____
Contribution from Trust	_____	_____	_____	_____
Utilities	_____	_____	_____	_____
Postage	_____	_____	_____	_____
Insurance	_____	_____	_____	_____

Scholarships ‗‗‗‗ ‗‗‗‗ ‗‗‗‗ ‗‗‗‗

Total Expenses ‗‗‗‗ ‗‗‗‗ ‗‗‗‗ ‗‗‗‗
Income

Interest
Fundraiser
Phone
Secretary
Meals
Newsletter
Other
Income
Bequests/Donations
Other
Fundraisers

Total Income _____ _____ _____ _____

INCOME LESS EXPENSES _____ _____ _____ _____

TAB 4: OFFICERS

The Lodge elects a Master, Senior Warden, Junior Warden, Secretary and Treasurer. So you cannot actually select these officers. However, most Lodges do have a presumed "line of succession," which gives you some idea of who the next year's officers may be.

During your year as Senior Warden, you should consider who will work best with you, giving due respect to the line of succession and the opinions of Past Masters and other leaders of your Lodge. You should discuss with your brethren the roles they may wish to play in the Lodge to form a team that is ready to move your Lodge forward. Forms are included to give you an opportunity to consider the present line of officers and then to project the line officers you expect to work with during your year as Master. The officer job descriptions in this book are intended for you to copy and distribute to your officers and officer candidates, to give them a concept of the responsibilities of the office.

Duties and Obligations of Lodge Officers

The officers of a Lodge have been elected or appointed to serve the Lodge because of their particular talents. Some are more gifted in certain areas than others, but all of them must possess one very important characteristic, that of devotion to duty. When a man accepts an office in a Masonic Lodge, he is saying to the brethren of his Lodge that he has committed himself to Masonry and to the complete fulfillment of his office. He should, prior to acceptance of an office, study the charges which will be made to him at his installation. He should also recognize that he will have to make certain sacrifices, as the job of an officer is not a one or two night a month obligation. There is a great deal of planning, studying, and attending involved in each of these offices. If he is not prepared to make these sacrifices, then he is not being fair to his Lodge or to himself by accepting the office. Every officer must work with enthusiasm, not only at his own job in the Lodge, but he must assist all other officers in the performance of their duties. By doing his job well, the officer is earning his way to the next office in line, or to some other position of responsibility in his Lodge.

The Senior Warden must be on the alert for potential line officers. Upon becoming Master of his Lodge, it will be his responsibility to appoint at least one member to the officer line. In the supervision of Degrees, committees and other Lodge functions, the Senior Warden will observe the members at work. He will also have the opportunity to delegate responsibility to members, which may bring to light good potential officers.

A successful Lodge has good ritual work, a good educational program, and good Lodge administration and management. It is the responsibility of every officer to see that your Lodge is a successful Lodge.

OFFICERS - your year as WORSHIPFUL MASTER

Year _____

Office	Member	Phone
Worshipful Master		
Junior Warden		
Senior Warden		
Treasurer		
Secretary		
Chaplain		
Senior Deacon		
Junior Deacon		
Senior Steward		
Junior Steward		
Tyler		

Marshal   _____   _____

Master Educator   _____   _____

Master of Ceremonies   _____   _____

Master of the Work (Ritual)   _____   _____

Lodge Trustee   _____   _____

Lodge Trustee   _____   _____

Lodge Trustee   _____   _____

Lodge Trustee   _____   _____

Lodge Trustee   _____   _____

_____   _____   _____

_____   _____   _____

_____   _____   _____

_____   _____   _____

_____   _____   _____

_____   _____   _____

_____   _____   _____

_____   _____   _____

Other Contacts

Title	Name	Phone
_____	_____	_____
_____	_____	_____
_____	_____	_____
_____	_____	_____
_____	_____	_____
_____	_____	_____
_____	_____	_____
_____	_____	_____
_____	_____	_____

_____   _____   _____
_____   _____   _____
_____   _____   _____
_____   _____   _____
_____   _____   _____
_____   _____   _____
_____   _____   _____
_____   _____   _____
_____   _____   _____
_____   _____   _____
_____   _____   _____

TAB 5: COMMITTEES

The development of committees is an important and challenging part of leadership. committees can make the members feel involved and can dramatically reduce your workload.

Initially, you should concern yourself with deciding what committees will be necessary to achieve your objectives. Then, you should consider who in your Lodge would be best to lead that committee. This should be accomplished at least one month prior to your installation, in order that you can announce the committees at your installation and let them get started right away. It rarely works to ask for volunteers.

Men will help only if they have the time and feel passionate about what you are trying to accomplish. If you want people to help you, you will probably have to ask them.

To effectively manage committees:

(1) Determine whom you want to chair the committee.

(2) Meet with that individual and explain to him clearly and specifically what you want done and how you want it done. Then ask him if he will do it.

(3) After you have found a committee chairman, with his input, determine who can best work and serve on the committee. Meet with each prospective committeeman individually, describe the committee to them and ask if they will serve with the chairman on the committee.

(4) Require periodic reports and updates from your chairmen. (That way, you'll never be caught unaware.)

(5) Give chairmen the freedom and support to do the job their way. The more effective you are in selecting, overseeing and empowering your committees, the more they will accomplish.

STANDING (or REGULAR) COMMITTEES

Standing Committees are those regular committees required by the By-Laws of the Lodge. They consist normally of three members. The Worshipful Master and the Wardens are "ex officio" members, or members by nature of their position. These committees will vary from Lodge to Lodge and jurisdiction to jurisdiction, but here are some standard Masonic Standing Committees:

Audit (and Budget) Committee, whose duty it shall be to audit the books, vouchers, records, and all reports of the Treasurer and Secretary, and report fully thereon at a stated meeting in January (or as Stated in your Lodge's By-Laws), and at such other times as the Worshipful Master may direct.

Charity Committee, consisting of three members of the Lodge, who shall have authority during recess of the Lodge to expend not more than Two Hundred Fifty ($250.00) Dollars for that purpose, or the amount specified by your Lodge. The Committee should examine all claimants for charity, if the Lodge deems it necessary.

Conduct Committee, consisting of three members of the Lodge, whose duty it shall be to take cognizance of the brethren within the jurisdiction of the Lodge, reconcile differences which may arise among Brethren, and when proper, prepare and prefer charges to the Lodge for its action.

Visiting Committee, whose duty it shall be to visit sick and distressed Brethren and their families, and sick and distressed widows and orphans of deceased Brethren, and report their findings to the Worshipful Master and the Lodge.

Inquisitorial Committee, whose duty it shall be to interview each prospective candidate from whom a petition for initiation has been received, and obtain from him such information relative to his motives and fitness as may be advisable. No ballot on such petition shall be taken until after said committee has reported thereon. The Master may also appoint a special Investigative Committee to conduct investigations on a candidate-by-candidate basis in lieu of using the Inquisitorial Committee.

SPECIAL (or IRREGULAR) COMMITTEES

Special Committees are those regular committees needed, but not required by the By-Laws of the Lodge. They consist normally of three members, appointed by the Worshipful Master. The Worshipful Master and the Wardens are "ex officio" members, or members by nature of their position. Here are examples of Special Committees:

Communications Committee, consisting of three members of the Lodge, who shall have the responsibility for publishing the online monthly newsletter, The Rockford Trestleboard; maintenance of the Lodge website; preparation and distribution of the Quarterly Update mail outs; and, procurement, implementation and maintenance of any other communications and communications processes as determined by the Lodge.

Long-Range Planning Committee, whose duty it shall be to ensure the Lodge completes the annual Long-Range Goals Checklist; prepares Grand Lodge awards registration forms for qualifying members; and sees that the Grand Lodge Long-Range Planning Committee goals are attained.

Masonic Education Committee, whose duty it shall be to educate and inform new members into the fraternity about the customs and uses of Masonry; prepare and administer a Lodge

Masonic Education and Information Program; ensure new candidates receive ritualistic instruction; and, see the new member and his family are integrated into the Lodge Family. This Committee is also responsible for the training of newly-elected officers, registration of new members in the Grand Lodge correspondence course programs, and general Masonic education.

Investigative Committee, whose duty it shall be to interview each prospective candidate from whom a petition for initiation has been received, and obtain from him such information relative to his motives and fitness as may be advisable. No ballot on such petition shall be taken until after said committee has reported thereon. This Committee shall consist of three Master Masons, and may be appointed on a candidate-by-candidate basis by the Worshipful Master.

D.A.D. Program, whose duty it is to support and encourage members to participate in the Dime-A-Day Annual Giving Program to provide additional Lodge funding for projects not covered by the General Fund.

Funeral Service Committee, who duty it is to arrange Masonic Funerals and associated details for deceased Brethren at the request of the family.

Trustee Committee, whose duty it is to perform all duties generally expected of such officers. It shall be their duty to see that the Lodge building, grounds and equipment are maintained, and to serve as legal signers of contracts made by the Lodge in legal session.

Other Committees, as needed or required and appointed by the Worshipful Master

A SIMPLIFIED COMMITTEE PROGRAM FOR YOUR YEAR

The following outline is a proposed, yet simplified, annual committee program for use with your Lodge. All to often, smaller Lodges suffer from the "Committee Plague." Too many committees will deter progress, accomplish nothing, and drive you mad as Worshipful Master. Simplify the process for yourself, so that you may concentrate your efforts in other areas that will be more beneficial. *The more committees you have, the less you will accomplish.*

STRATEGIC PLANNING COMMITTEE

Chaired by the Worshipful Master, this Committee has six main functions:

1. Developing a Master Plan: The Committee will look five to seven years in the future to forecast trends and identify opportunities. The Committee will advise the Lodge what it can expect in terms of membership, finances, and expenditures. It will identify the issues the Lodge will need to confront, the problems the Worshipful Master will need to solve, and the programs that will have to be put in place. The first time around, the Committee will propose a strategic plan. In subsequent years, it will evaluate the plan; propose revisions as appropriate, and track progress toward implementing the plan.

2. Raising Money: The Committee will periodically assess the adequacy of the dues structure against needs, encourage and design gift programs with suitable incentives (buy a chair, be recognized on a wall plaque), encourage and facilitate trusts and bequests, promote perpetual memberships for existing and deceased members, and develop ideas for raising funds.

3. Investing Funds: The Committee will review investment options (CD, Ginny Mae funds, other investments), and review how much or little risk should be tolerated in the context of fiduciary responsibilities to safeguard Lodge funds.

4. Apportioning Money: The Committee will review existing budgets, suggest ways to promote greater efficiency, and suggest setting up dedicated funds, for example, for Masonic charity, scholarships, building repair, and capital improvements.

5. Prioritizing Expenditures: The Committee will establish repair and capital improvement priorities and suggest a spending plan. Because of the nature of its charter, this Committee should be chaired by the Worshipful Master and includes the Trustees, the Secretary, and Treasurer. Other officers and members should be encouraged to attend and participate in the deliberations.

6. Performing Lodge Audits. The Audit Sub-Committee will review annually or periodically the Administrative and Financial status and activities of the Lodge as needed or required and report the findings to the Committee.

Members:

(1) Governing Members: WM, SW, JW, Treasurer, Secretary
(2) Audit Sub-Committee: Experienced Past Master, Immediate Past Master, Senior Warden, Junior Warden, Treasurer, Secretary
(3) Trustees

LABOR & WORK COMMITTEE

Chaired by the Senior Warden, this Committee will be responsible for a variety of activities essential to the proper functioning of the Lodge. These include:

1. Grounds and Facilities Maintenance.
2. Investigation of Petitioners.
3. Lecture Instruction.
4. Lodge Ritual Instruction
5. Lodge Leadership and Education Programs
6. Community Service Projects, Events & Activities
7. Inter-Lodge Activities & Visitation
8. Promote/Coordinate Activities with Non-Masonic Groups & Organizations

The Committee should include Past Masters, the Master of the Work, Master Educator, and other experienced Masons who have responsibility for the five functions listed above, as well as other brethren with skills in these areas of Lodge operations.

Members:

(1) Governing Members: SW (Chair), SD, JD
(2) Grounds & Facilities Sub-Committee: SW (Chair), Lodge Safety Officer/Building Supervisor, Grounds Supervisor
(3) Investigative Sub-Committee: Senior Deacon (Chair), Junior Deacon, Tyler, Marshal
(4) Masonic Education Sub-Committee: Master Educator (Chair), Master of the Work
(5) Oversight Sub-Committee: Senior Active PM (Chair), All Past Masters
(6) Ritual Sub-Committee: Master of the Work (Chair), Degree Captains, Proficiency/Lecture Card Holders
(7)Labor Operations Sub-Committee: Assisting Brethren

REFRESHMENT COMMITTEE

Chaired by: Junior Warden

This Committee has three main functions:

1. Promoting Masonic Family Activities: The Committee will work with all of the organizations that meet at the Lodge to plan, coordinate, and jointly support each other's activities. The Committee also will have responsibility for Family & Awards Night, Wives and Widows Luncheon, Ice Cream Social, Masonic Support for OES and DeMolay Events, and other similar events. It will promote visits to the shut-in and elderly, contributions for the Widows & Orphans Fund, and take charge of running fundraising activities as directed by the Strategic Planning Committee. It will promote attendance at the installations of Masonic Family organizations, schedule family and youth programs at the Lodge, run the Child ID programs, etc.

2. Promoting Activities with the Families of Masons: The Committee also will plan activities that Masons can share, as Masons, with their own families. It is important that there be regular occasions for brethren to get together socially that will

interest and involve wives and family. One possibility is a monthly "meet and socialize" night where interested Masons and their wives can come to the Lodge, for example, on a Saturday night, and those who show up can decide on a restaurant to attend or a movie to see. This Committee is chaired by the Junior Warden, and includes the Stewards, the Chaplain, the Marshal and a number of other active members. Close involvement of the Junior Warden with the brethren and their spouses, and with Masonic Family activities, will ensure that he is well known and increase the amount of support he can expect when he becomes Worshipful Master. Obviously, there should be coordinators appointed for each activity or event. But by centralizing and focusing all of our social and fundraising activities in a single committee, the Lodge can better assist all of the coordinators, ensure that they are not working in isolation, or worse yet, at cross purposes, and can promote and develop synergy between all of the planned activities.

3. Coordination of Lodge Meals Served for Masonic Functions: The Junior Warden, assisted by the Stewards and the Knife & Fork Committee will be responsible for coordinating all meals and light refreshments served at the Lodge for Masonic Functions, e.g., Stated Meetings, Degree Work, Officer & Special Meetings, etc.

Members:

(1) Governing Members: JW (CHAIR), SS, JS
(2) Chaplain, Marshal, Treasurer
(3) Knife & Fork Committee: SS, 3 newest Master Masons
(4) Appendant & Concordant Bodies Liaisons
(5) Refreshment Operations Sub-Committee: Assisting Brethren⁊

CHARITY & BENEVOLENCE COMMITTEE

Chaired by: Treasurer

This Committee will be responsible for a variety of activities essential to meeting the charity and benevolence needs of the Lodge. These include:

1. Charity Fund Operations
2. Benevolence Activities
3. Lodge Samaritan Program Administration
4. Charitable Grants to Outside Entities
5. Charitable Fundraising
6. Masonic Charities Contributions
7. Funeral Service Coordination

The Committee should include the Charity Steward, whose job it is to promote Charitable activities and events, coordinate Charity Fund disbursements, serve as liaison with outside individuals, groups and organizations concerning charity issues; and, the Lodge Almoner, whose job it is to coordinate all benevolence issues (gifts, Widow's Baskets, Funeral issues, Flowers, etc.) Committee will consist of Past Masters and other experienced Masons who have had experience and responsibility in the areas listed above, as well as other brethren with skills in these areas of Lodge operations.

Members:

(1) Governing Members: Treasurer, Charity Steward, Almoner
(2) Funeral Service Sub-Committee
(3) Charity Operations Sub-Committee: Assisting Brethren

☐

MEMBERSHIP COMMITTEE

Chaired by the Senior Deacon, this Committee has four main functions:

1. Obtaining New Members: The Committee will ensure that all Masons know how to use the Grand Lodge publications, and know how to approach potential members and interest them in our fraternity. The Committee will help to educate Masons in the history and traditions of Freemasonry so they understand what to say to a non-Mason to explain what the Fraternity is all about and what the Lodge does. The Committee will be responsible for Lodge public relations so that Lodge activities come to community attention, and be responsible for the "Bring-A-Friend" nights.

2. Keeping in Close Contact with Members and Widows: The Committee will be responsible for institution of a telephone system that not only serves to alert the brethren when there is a funeral or other emergency, but also ensures that each member and widow is called at least once every month. This should be a short call to keep in contract, to check on health, to see if assistance is needed, and to simply find out more about the brother or widow.

3. Reactivating Inactive Members: The regular calls will reestablish a relationship between the inactive Mason and the Lodge. At a minimum, the Lodge will know when the brother is ill and can send a card or provide other assistance. The brother can likely be encouraged to attend Lodge two to four times a year. And learning about the brother's available time and talents will enable the Worshipful Master and Lodge officers to find a place for the brother on a committee or to enlist him to share his interests and experiences with the Lodge, for example, by putting on a Lodge program or giving a talk. The Committee, as a result of its calls and contacts, will report on the widows, on sickness and distress, and can make every meeting a "Bring-a-Mason" night. In addition, this Committee should reach out to sojourners and ensure that visitors to the Lodge are truly made welcome and comfortable, and not left alone and isolated in the social hall. This Committee should be chaired by the Senior Deacon, and include a mixture of older and newer members. Older Masons will know many of the Lodge brethren and can be on your "telephone subcommittee," newer Masons can be a good source of petitions, and by involving them actively on this Committee, they will quickly become acquainted with other members of the Lodge.

4. Conduct of Members: The Conduct Sub-Committee will handle all conduct issues between the members and recommend any corrective action to be taken to the Committee.

Members:

(1) Governing Members: SD (CHAIR), JD, Secretary, Tyler, Marshal
(2) Communications Sub-Committee
(3) Conduct Sub-Committee
(4) Membership Operations Sub-Committee: Assisting Brethren

Lodge Committee Roster

Type: ___STANDING ___SPECIAL

Name of Committee_____

Purpose of Committee_____

Goals for Committee:

1. by _____ (date), to accomplish:

_____

_____

_____

2. by _____ (date), to accomplish:

_____

_____

_____

3. by _____ (date), to accomplish:

_____

_____

_____

Chairman of Committee_____Phone_____

Committee Member_____Phone_____

Committee Member_____Phone_____

Additional Members, if needed:

Committee Member_____Phone_____

Committee Member_____Phone_____

Lodge Committee Roster

Type: ___STANDING ___SPECIAL

Name of Committee_____

Purpose of Committee_____

Goals for Committee:

1. by _____ (date), to accomplish:

_____

_____

_____

2. by _____ (date), to accomplish:

_____

_____

_____

3. by _____ (date), to accomplish:

_____

_____

_____

Chairman of Committee_____Phone_____

Committee Member_____Phone_____

Committee Member_____Phone_____

Additional Members, if needed:

Committee Member_____Phone_____

Committee Member_____Phone_____

Lodge Committee Roster

Type: ___STANDING ___SPECIAL

Name of Committee_____

Purpose of Committee_____

Goals for Committee:

1. by _____ (date), to accomplish:

_____

_____

_____

2. by _____ (date), to accomplish:

_____

_____

_____

3. by _____ (date), to accomplish:

_____

_____

_____

Chairman of Committee_____Phone_____

Committee Member_____Phone_____

Committee Member_____Phone_____

Additional Members, if needed:

Committee Member_____Phone_____

Committee Member_____Phone_____

Lodge Committee Roster

Type: ___STANDING ___SPECIAL

Name of Committee_____

Purpose of Committee_____

Goals for Committee:

1. by _____ (date), to accomplish:

_____

_____

_____

2. by _____ (date), to accomplish:

_____

_____

_____

3. by _____ (date), to accomplish:

_____

_____

_____

Chairman of Committee_____Phone_____

Committee Member_____Phone_____

Committee Member_____Phone_____

Additional Members, if needed:

Committee Member_____Phone_____

Committee Member_____Phone_____

Lodge Committee Roster

Type: ___STANDING ___SPECIAL

Name of Committee_____

Purpose of Committee_____

Goals for Committee:

1. by _____ (date), to accomplish:

_____

_____

_____

2. by _____ (date), to accomplish:

_____

_____

_____

3. by _____ (date), to accomplish:

_____

_____

_____

Chairman of Committee_____Phone_____

Committee Member_____Phone_____

Committee Member_____Phone_____

Additional Members, if needed:

Committee Member_____Phone_____

Committee Member_____Phone_____

Lodge Committee Roster

Type: ___STANDING ___SPECIAL

Name of Committee_____

Purpose of Committee_____

Goals for Committee:

1. by _____ (date), to accomplish:

_____

_____

_____

2. by _____ (date), to accomplish:

_____

_____

_____

3. by _____ (date), to accomplish:

_____

_____

_____

Chairman of Committee_____Phone_____

Committee Member_____Phone_____

Committee Member_____Phone_____

Additional Members, if needed:

Committee Member_____Phone_____

Committee Member_____Phone_____

Lodge Committee Roster

Type: ___STANDING ___SPECIAL

Name of Committee_____

Purpose of Committee_____

Goals for Committee:

1. by _____ (date), to accomplish:

_____

_____

_____

2. by _____ (date), to accomplish:

_____

_____

_____

3. by _____ (date), to accomplish:

_____

_____

_____

Chairman of Committee_____Phone_____

Committee Member_____Phone_____

Committee Member_____Phone_____

Additional Members, if needed:

Committee Member_____Phone_____

Committee Member_____Phone_____

Lodge Committee Roster

Type: ___STANDING ___SPECIAL

Name of Committee_____

Purpose of Committee_____

Goals for Committee:

1. by _____ (date), to accomplish:

_____

_____

_____

2. by _____ (date), to accomplish:

_____

_____

_____

3. by _____ (date), to accomplish:

_____

_____

_____

Chairman of Committee_____Phone_____

Committee Member_____Phone_____

Committee Member_____Phone_____

Additional Members, if needed:

Committee Member_____Phone_____

Committee Member_____Phone_____

Lodge Committee Roster

Type: ___STANDING ___SPECIAL

Name of Committee_____

Purpose of Committee_____

Goals for Committee:

1. by _____ (date), to accomplish:

_____

_____

_____

2. by _____ (date), to accomplish:

_____

_____

_____

3. by _____ (date), to accomplish:

_____

_____

_____

Chairman of Committee_____Phone_____

Committee Member_____Phone_____

Committee Member_____Phone_____

Additional Members, if needed:

Committee Member_____Phone_____

Committee Member_____Phone_____

Lodge Committee Roster

Type: ___STANDING ___SPECIAL

Name of Committee_____

Purpose of Committee_____

Goals for Committee:

1. by _____ (date), to accomplish:

_____

_____

_____

2. by _____ (date), to accomplish:

_____

_____

_____

3. by _____ (date), to accomplish:

_____

_____

_____

Chairman of Committee_____Phone_____

Committee Member_____Phone_____

Committee Member_____Phone_____

Additional Members, if needed:

Committee Member_____Phone_____

Committee Member_____Phone_____

Lodge Committee Roster

Type: ___STANDING ___SPECIAL

Name of Committee_____

Purpose of Committee_____

Goals for Committee:

1. by _____ (date), to accomplish:

_____

_____

_____

2. by _____ (date), to accomplish:

_____

_____

_____

3. by _____ (date), to accomplish:

_____

_____

_____

Chairman of Committee_____Phone_____

Committee Member_____Phone_____

Committee Member_____Phone_____

Additional Members, if needed:

Committee Member_____Phone_____

Committee Member_____Phone_____

Lodge Committee Roster

Type: ___STANDING ___SPECIAL

Name of Committee_____

Purpose of Committee_____

Goals for Committee:

1. by _____ (date), to accomplish:

_____

_____

_____

2. by _____ (date), to accomplish:

_____

_____

_____

3. by _____ (date), to accomplish:

_____

_____

_____

Chairman of Committee_____Phone_____

Committee Member_____Phone_____

Committee Member_____Phone_____

Additional Members, if needed:

Committee Member_____Phone_____

Committee Member_____Phone_____

Lodge Committee Roster

Type: ___STANDING   ___SPECIAL

Name of Committee_____

Purpose of Committee_____

Goals for Committee:

1. by _____ (date), to accomplish:

_____

_____

_____

2. by _____ (date), to accomplish:

_____

_____

_____

3. by _____ (date), to accomplish:

_____

_____

_____

Chairman of Committee_____Phone_____

Committee Member_____Phone_____

Committee Member_____Phone_____

Additional Members, if needed:

Committee Member_____Phone_____

Committee Member_____Phone_____

Lodge Committee Roster

Type: ___STANDING ___SPECIAL

Name of Committee_____

Purpose of Committee_____

Goals for Committee:

1. by _____ (date), to accomplish:

_____

_____

_____

2. by _____ (date), to accomplish:

_____

_____

_____

3. by _____ (date), to accomplish:

_____

_____

_____

Chairman of Committee_____Phone_____

Committee Member_____Phone_____

Committee Member_____Phone_____

Additional Members, if needed:

Committee Member_____Phone_____

Committee Member_____Phone_____

TAB 6: LODGE MEMBERS

This is where you should keep a copy of the membership roster, so you can have a quick way to contact the members of your Lodge. If your Lodge has a calling committee, this would also be a good place to keep information about that program. E-mail is a wonderful tool for this purpose. You should ask for a member's current e-mail address in the annual dues notice.

This can also be a good place for you to keep track of newer members and candidates for degrees.

Both should receive special attention for the first year or two of their membership to ensure they feel involved and welcome!

Older members of the Lodge may need to be called. Newer members can be involved in the process of calling the old members.

Ideas for Member Recruitment/Retention in Masonry

Idea	X
Give a special incentive to top line signers of new petitioners (Pins, clothing, certificates etc.).	
Plan a Guest Night for potential candidates.	
Identify your most at-risk members and target them for additional contact.	
Do a member survey of your least active members. Let those who respond know that you are listening to them by telling them that you will try to do what they suggested on the survey.	
Get members involved in focus groups by email or blogs (new members may prefer this type of involvement.)	
Send out a monthly email newsletter that is sent out simultaneously with the mailed publication.	
Along with the Mentor Program, have a New Member Designated Contact group.	
Contact top line signers from the previous year. Thank them and ask them for continued involvement with the new candidate. Ask them to continue with new member	

recruitment.	
Develop a new member newsletter and send it out quarterly to all members who have been raised within the last year. Include educational materials as well as an up-to-date calendar and incentives to become involved (except for the calendar, the same correspondence can be used each year).	
Create a new member section on your website.	
Develop a list of your (most wanted) delinquent or dropped new members and ask lodge officers to make personal appeals to reconsider their membership. Consider calling their "Top Line Signer". Make a time line to get the results to the Master.	
On the night when a petition is to be voted on, ask the petitioner to be available. If he is elected, call him and have him meet with the brothers after the meeting to be congratulated.	
Send a "How Are We Doing?" survey to new members six months after they are raised. If they don't return them, give them a call.	
Create a "thank you" list which includes the names and contributions of active members. Place this list in your newsletter, on your website, and read it in open lodge.	
Ask individual Past Masters to be liaisons with other Masonic organizations and to regularly report their activities in open lodge.	
Send a special communication and possibly a small token gift to each brother who lives out of town thanking them for their continued participation and loyalty to your Lodge. Make up Lodge pens, vehicle decals, cups or maybe key chains as gifts.	
Assign new members to make detailed notes on Guest Nights, fund raisers, community activities, and social events. Save those notes in a computer file to be used for future planning references.	
Announce a membership goal of getting one new member for every twenty-five (25) members each year.	
Publish a summary of important highlights from the Grand Lodge session and Area Conferences on the lodge's website and newsletter.	
To promote attendance at a future meeting, publish an interview and/or biography with the featured speaker in the	

newsletter and/or on your website.	
Find out what ideas are working for other organizations and discuss them at officers' meetings.	
Make a file of those members who have dropped their membership in years past and send them a "We Want You Back" letter. Include the reasons they have dropped in the file.	
Designate one officer to closely monitor brothers who are shut-ins or who are hospitalized.	
Never have officers' meetings before a regular stated meeting but, instead, direct your officers to socialize with all of the attendees.	
The Master should occasionally meet with your Sr. and Jr. Wardens alone and discuss lodge issues to be sure all are on the same page.	
Appoint a communications chair and direct him to make and submit news releases to the local press with photographs immediately following installations, community projects, and unique lodge activities. He should also submit articles concerning upcoming fund raisers.	
Hold a "Fathers & Sons Night" (Perhaps in conjunction with other Lodges).	
Ask officers and active members to relate their most valued Masonic experiences or benefits and use those statements as quotes for recruitment and retention purposes.	
Place a downloadable petition on your Lodge web site.	
Keep an eye on Grand Lodge publications. Look for up-coming dates and successful ideas from other lodges.	
Ask your District Representative to report on successful events at other Lodges.	
Send hand-written notes to the chairman of lodge events thanking them for their service.	
Assign the task of taking an inventory of promotional Masonic brochures and other publications. Make note when supplies are low and have them replenished when appropriate.	
Get new members nametags ASAP so that they can be recognized at a glance. Make sure the name is in large print.	
Assign new members to minor management and planning positions as soon as possible and identify one person (or persons) they can call for advice and help.	

Hold a "town meeting" for the general membership to show that the leadership really cares about their concerns and ideas.	
Make an annual safety inspection of the lodge building and repair problem areas.	
Consider installing a first-aid kit and possibly a defibrillator. Ask the new Brothers to help you.	
Have name tags available at events such as dinners so members get to know other members and spouses. Select a group of less active members as a focus group and give the group a specific task.	
Check the answering service on the lodge phone regularly for calls from potential members. If no message service, get one installed.	
Ask one Past Master per month to write an article about his experiences for the newsletter.	
Get on the mailing list of other lodges in your area.	
Develop a "Congratulations" message you can send to members who have taken positions in other Masonic organizations or have been promoted in their personal life.	
Interview new members and ask them why they joined. Use this information as an insight for future recruitment programs.	
Copy newspaper or other publication articles that mention your lodge in a favorable way and include them in your newsletter.	
Invite Brothers to speak at a dinner on non-Masonic topics such as their professions.	
Ask the secretary to create and send out a "Thanks for Renewing Your Membership" letter or card to each NPD when they pay their dues.	
Have secretary send "welcome and thank you for joining" letter or card to new members.	
IMMEDIATELY send the candidate registration form to the Grand Lodge office when received. Include their mailing information as well as their mentor contact information. This form is the detachable form on the blue petition and, when sent in, the candidate will receive a quantity of great information from the Grand Lodge Secretary.	
Read any and all communications from the Grand Lodge Membership and Leadership committees at each lodge officers'	

meeting.	
Report updates of membership goals on the website, in the newsletter and in lodge.	
Play Grand Lodge Membership videos at lodge meetings two or three times a year and discuss them.	
Supply each newly raised Mason with a DVD from the Grand Lodge entitled "What Every New Mason Should Know."	
Conduct a practice "investigative interview" at a stated communication and discuss how to use this interview as the beginning of the bonding process for the new candidate.	
Attend Masters and Wardens meetings to find out what other lodges are doing for membership retention and recruitment activities.	
Have the Master's wife, or another informed officer's spouse, send a letter of welcome to the new petitioner's wife offering to answer her questions about the Fraternity.	
Invite top line signers of petitions to be special guests at a lodge meeting. Pay for their meal and have the Master ask them to sit in the East with him.	
Make sure that every new Brother has SOMETHING TO DO AND SOMETHING TO LEARN.	
Remember to invite all petitioners to any dinners or events that are open to the public. This should include dinners held before stated meetings. Host a get-together for member's wives and the wives of newly raised brothers as well as the wives of petitioners.	
Make a list of former active members who have not attended within the last year and develop a process to encourage them to attend in the future.	
Construct a bulletin board containing photos and information and on new members and have it placed as you enter the lodge so that all brothers can identify and greet them properly.	
When someone is ill or has to miss a Lodge meeting, give him a call, write a note or send an e-mail.	
Provide an occasional questionnaire to get feedback from members. If problems or dissatisfactions are detected, take steps to fix it.	
Involve all members in setting realistic and creative membership goals. People who participate in setting some of	

the objectives are more committed to reaching the goal.	
Keep in touch with inactive and former brothers through invitations to social events and a yearly update on Lodge news and events.	
Have a social gathering for all members who have joined your Lodge within the past 12 months. It's an opportunity for newer members to ask questions, share experiences, and get to know each other on a more personal basis.	
Find the most capable, most enthusiastic and dynamic person you can for your Membership Chairman and treat him well.	
Make it a big deal when a new member is qualified to move on to the next degree. Give him some type of award.	
Encourage periodic spouse activities to help insure support at home.	
Adopt a sister Lodge in another jurisdiction. Ask a new brother to correspond with that Lodge and make report to your Lodge.	
Recognition helps retain members. Create some goofy awards, i.e. "best ad lib ritual award".	
Send a news release about a member's Masonic accomplishments to his company's newsletter. If a brother is promoted in his job, mention it in the Lodge newsletter.	
Sponsor a DeMolay Chapter or Jobs Daughters Bethel and encourage their fathers to join.	
Be committed to ritual excellence.	
Keep a positive attitude; it increases energy and each member's self-esteem.	
Become more community minded. Become actively involved with a local charity and make it an annual event.	
Give members worthwhile jobs and then let them do them. Involve lots of brothers to avoid burning out the brothers who always volunteer to carry the load.	
Find unique ways to give more individual recognition to those brothers who deserve it.	
Encourage members to give periodic testimonials about what membership means to them.	
Encourage attendance at Area Conferences and the Grand Lodge Annual Session.	
Find creative ways to provide financial support for members who attend.	

Call absent members, letting them know they're missed without making them feel guilty.	
Keep an updated Lodge roster in the hands of all members with current phone numbers, addresses and e-mail addresses.	
Provide a yearly calendar to all members and have it ready before your Annual Installation.	
Send cards and flowers to those who are ill, have had a recent death in the family, or have something to celebrate, such as marriage, a new baby, or some other special occasion. Have some appropriate cards on hand for such occasions.	
Allow a Lodge member to drop his membership without making him feel guilty.	
Do something every year for your Masonic Widows.	
Consider giving a scholarship to the child or grandchild of one of your deceased members. Have a new brother make the contact.	
Make personal contact with those brothers who did not complete their degree work.	
Keep your Lodge building clean, attractive and well maintained. Plan a cleanup day and have the new Brothers help.	
Make a special effort to pick up older members for Lodge meetings.	
Consider buying matching Masonic shirts, caps or ties. (It's a group thing)	
Take a part of each meeting to openly discuss what purpose the brothers want to fulfill as a Lodge and how they want to proceed in accomplishing their goals.	
Share your Lodge hall with other Non-Profit organizations in the community and invite those organizations to your lodge's fund raisers and public events.	
Invite other Masonic organizations to give presentations at your Lodge.	
Have one formal meeting each month and one "special activity" meeting.	
Conduct a kids ID event and have a knowledgeable brother available to answer membership questions.	

Suggested Lodge Annual Work Plan

This work plan has, in part, been adapted and expanded for use with permission of the Grand Lodge of Tennessee, F.&A.M., from their Vision 2013 Program:

SECTION 1--MANAGEMENT	X
Does your Lodge have some means of regular communication with its membership, i.e. a monthly or quarterly newsletter? Is it distributed to your Widows, E.A.'s and/or F.C.'s	
Does your Lodge have an OPEN INSTALLATION OF OFFICERS?	
Do all your Lodge officers attend at least one District Meeting this year?	
Do all your Lodge officers attend at least one Grand Lecturer's SCHOOL OF INSTRUCTION this year?	
Do all your Lodge officers attend at least one Grand Lecturer's OFFICIAL VISIT this year?	
Will your Lodge be represented at the annual Grand Lodge Communication by your stationed officers and/or your Secretary this year?	
Does your Lodge have an assigned committee for oversight or implementation of the Grand Lodge Annual Work Program OR does it have a LONG RANGE PLANNING COMMIMTTEE?	

Does your Lodge conduct a regular scheduled leadership educational program for your officers?	
Will any of your officers attend a training session conducted by the GRAND LODGE EDUCATION COMMITTEE?	
Does your Lodge conduct a regular scheduled educational program for ritual?	
Does your Lodge conduct a regular scheduled educational program for other than ritual (Masonic History, Code etc.)?	
Does your Lodge utilize videos and other paraphernalia from the Grand Lodge in its training, including orientation of new or prospective members?	
Does your Lodge have a regular building and grounds clean-up program with supervision?	
Does your Lodge have an internet home page?	
Can your Lodge confer all sections of all 3 degrees from memory using only your members?	
Does your Lodge have at least one brother who can conduct a Masonic Funeral from memory?	
Will your Lodge apply for any Masonic achievement awards this year?	
SECTION 2--MEMBERSHIP	
Will your Lodge hold a special meeting to recognize Past Masters this year?	
Will your Lodge hold a special meeting to recognize 25 and 50 year members and/or an "Old Timer's Night" this year?	
Does your Lodge sponsor a DeMolay, Rainbow Chapter or a Job's Daughters Bethel?	
Will your Lodge have an Open House for the community or a community group (e.g. Chamber of Commerce, elected officials, pastors, scout leaders etc.)?	
Does your Lodge have a formal orientation program for new members?	
Does your Lodge assign a "buddy" or some specific individual to each new member to teach lectures etc.?	
Does your Lodge include the wives and family members of new or prospective members in the initial orientation?	
Does your Lodge serve refreshments at degrees, stated meetings and/or installations?	

Does your Lodge formally notify local newspapers and/or radio/TV stations about meetings and special events?	
How many of your Lodge members have earned a VOLUNTARY SERVICE AWARD?	
SECTION 3--FRATERNAL RELATIONS	
Will your Lodge hold a special meeting to recognize its Masonic Widows and Orphans this year?	
Does your Lodge present Grand Lodge Masonic Widows' pins to its widows?	
Does your Lodge present Blue Slipper pins to members' wives and/or daughters?	
Will your Lodge hold a special meeting to commemorate St. John's Day in June and/or December?	
Will your Lodge hold any type of special meetings designed for the inclusion of the ladies and/or children of the brethren (Christmas Party, family night etc.)?	
Will your Lodge hold any meeting or function jointly with one of the appendant bodies this year	
Will your Lodge visit another Masonic Lodge in this or any other Grand Jurisdiction this year for the purpose of conferring a Masonic Degree?	
Will your Lodge host another Masonic Lodge from this or any other Grand Jurisdiction this year for the purpose of conferring a Masonic Degree?	
Will your Lodge sponsor a trip to another Lodge in this or any other Grand Jurisdiction this year for any purpose other than conferring a Masonic Degree?	
Will your Lodge hold or participate in a special patriotic or veterans function this year?	
Will your Lodge recognize its outstanding member who has been a member for less than 2 years (rookie)? For more than 2 years (veteran)?	
SECTION 4--COMMUNITY INVOLVEMENT AND BENEVOLENCE	
Will your Lodge donate to or hold a special fund raising event this year to benefit the Masonic Widows and Orphans' Fund?	
Will your Lodge donate to the George Washington Masonic Memorial this year?	
Will your Lodge hold a special fund raising event or assist any	

other organization(s) in any fund raising event for charity this year?	
Will your Lodge hold or participate in a Masonic dedication this year?	
Will your Lodge participate in a HABITAT FOR HUMANITY project this year?	
Will your Lodge provide aid to a spousal abuse/domestic violence shelter this year?	
Will your Lodge provide aid to a public school library reading assistance program?	
Will your Lodge provide aid to a Masonic Service Association (MSA) program?	
Will your Lodge conduct a Child ID event this year?	
Will your Lodge sponsor a youth sports team this year?	
Will your Lodge participate in a highway clean-up and/or adopt-a-highway this year?	
Will your Lodge sponsor or work with a Boys' or Girls' Club and or Big Brothers/Sisters this year?	
Did your Lodge sponsor a 4-H club year?	
How many academic scholarships will your Lodge award this year?	
Will your Lodge participate in programs or event of interaction with the public school system this year? (Anti-drug, D.A.R.E., anti-crime, speech or essay contests, science fairs, reading programs etc.).	
Will your Lodge provide assistance to the welfare of a distressed brother, widow or orphan this year?	
Will your Lodge "loan" its facilities or equipment to a community group or church to facilitate their public or private event?	
Will your Lodge co-sponsor or joint venture a community event or project with another non-Masonic organization?	
Will your Lodge join in sponsorship of a Masonic county or district charity fund?	

SECTION 5--OTHER

In the spaces below, please describe any other activity(ies) your Lodge has conducted not addressed in any of the questions above:

Lodge TO DO List

NEVER HAVE MORE THAT TWO THINGS ON YOUR RADAR AT ONE TIME. List the things, by priority (most important first) that you would like to accomplish this year. Cross them off as they are completed. You WILL NOT under most circumstances, complete your list in your year as Worshipful Master, and SOME will fix themselves, When they do, DO NOT rehash the issue; move on.

Priority Task   TBC by date

_____ _____ _____

_____ _____ _____

_____ _____ _____

_____ _____ _____

_____ _____ _____

_____ _____ _____

_____ _____ _____

_____ _____ _____

_____ _____ _____

_____ _____ _____

_____ _____ _____

_____ _____ _____

_____ _____ _____

_____ _____ _____

_____ _____ _____

_____ _____ _____

_____ _____ _____

_____ _____ _____

5-YR Degree Work Statistics

MONTH	YEAR			YEAR			YEAR			YEAR			YEAR		
	EA	FC	MM	EA	FC	MM	EA	FC	MM	EA	FC	MM	EA	FC	MM
1															
2															
3															
4															
5															
6															
7															
8															
9															
10															
11															
12															
TOT															

5-YR New Master Mason Membership Goals
(G=Goal, A=Actual)

YEAR		YEAR		YEAR		YEAR		YEAR	
G	A	G	A	G	A	G	A	G	A

5-YR Lecture/Proficiency Card Holder Statistics

YEAR		YEAR		YEAR		YEAR		YEAR	
LEC	PRO	LEC	PRO	LEC	PRO	LEC	PRO	LEC	PRO

TAB 7: LODGE COMMUNICATIONS

One of the most important aspects of leading and managing your Lodge is to be in touch with your officers, Lodge members and other groups connected with the Lodge, such as Scottish and York Rites, DeMolay, Eastern Star, etc.

In this section, place a copy of all communications you send out. This could be your monthly newsletter to all members, a letter to your officers, a memo to the building committee or a request to Grand Lodge.

As you send out regular communications, include your District Chairman and Deputies, Grand Lecturer, the local Lodge Association, and Grand Lodge on your mailing list. These brothers are here to help you, and will be more able to help when they know what's happening in your Lodge.

TAB 8: OTHER COMMUNICATIONS

In this section, place all of the incoming communications you receive from various groups. Examples would be letters from Grand Lodge or the Grand Master, your District Chairman, District Deputies, the Grand Lodge Education Officer, Scottish Rite, York Rite, Shrine, Eastern Star, DeMolay, etc.

By keeping track of the activities of the various groups, you can minimize date conflicts for events at your Lodge and inform your Lodge of activities that may be of interest to them.

TAB 9: RESOURCES

Your year as Master of your Lodge will be challenging, but should also be enjoyable. Many of your brothers have been in your position and are able to help you work through the challenges and make the most of your time in the East. There are also many other resources, including books, tapes, and websites.

As Master "your powers are nigh unto absolute". Fortunately, that power usually exists only to the degree of support given to you by the officers in your Lodge. They are your first line of support. Talk to them regularly.

More importantly, listen to them regularly! Your next line is your Past Masters. They can help you with historical perspectives and how programs or ideas worked in the past. Take care to balance their advice with the needs of the current membership and activities of the Lodge. Other members of the Lodge can also help with developing ideas and programs.

From outside the Lodge, your first line of assistance is your District Deputy. He is a Past Master, and is familiar with other Lodges in your area and can provide information about their successful programs. The District Representative is the person with whom you should consult when you need help that no one in your Lodge can provide. He can help you with programs, ritual, information, etc. Other resource people include the Grand Secretary and your Grand Lecture. The Grand Lodge also has programs that are designed to help you.

Below is a list of items that are available. There are a lot of materials that can help you, but they will take time for you to digest. Clearly, preparing for your year as Master takes time. A benefit of being an officer in various stations is that those offices give you time to learn and prepare. The study of books and materials is time consuming, but learning is a major reason that a man becomes a Freemason. What you learn as a Lodge officer will help you later on in life.

SUGGESTED RESOURCES FOR LEADERSHIP

Masonic Lifeline: Leadership by Allen E. Roberts
This is a short, to the point book about the meaning of leadership within the Masonic Lodge and structure.

Key to Freemasonry's Growth by Allen E. Roberts
Another short and to the point book on various aspects of membership, retention and increases of membership.

Macoy's Worshipful Master's Assistant by Allen E. Roberts
This book provides a rounded perspective of all aspects of running a Lodge, including program ideas, jurisprudence, ceremonies, ritual, etc.

In Search of Leadership by Allen E. Roberts

Freemasonry At The Top by Beaumont
This book in particular is a very short, easily read book that provides great program ideas as well as specific information on when you should start planning for your year in the East.

Seven Habits of Highly Effective People

First Things First

Principled Centered Leadership by Stephen Covey
While these three books are not Masonic, they provide terrific insight on the meaning of leadership, how to lead people, how to be effective in your actions and activities.

SUGGESTED RESOURCES FOR LODGE ADMINISTRATION

Lodge Secretary's Handbook
This provides the Lodge Secretary with information he needs to work effectively with the Master, his Lodge and with Grand Lodge.

Jurisprudence of Freemasonry by Mackey If problems arise in your Lodge, this book will provide the information you need to handle some of those issues.

Masonic Lodge Methods by Blakemore.

How to Become a Masonic Lodge Officer by Haywood This book is especially good for the newly appointed officer. Information is provided on all the different places and stations of the Lodge.

Robert's Rules of Order
While the Grand Lodge of Tennessee does not necessarily run its meetings according to Robert's, you should be familiar with the parliamentary procedure, such as how to make a motion, seconding, discussion, voting, etc.

The Master's Book by Carl H. Claudy

The Worshipful Master's Workbook by Cabell F. Cobbs (M.S.A.)

Program Notebook for Worshipful Masters M.S.A.
A terrific pocket-sized book to help you plan your year. Questions and blank spaces are provided to help you determine your programs, officers, meetings, etc.

The Hat and Gavel M.S.A.

TAB 10: DEGREE WORK

DEGREE TEAMS

As your year as Master of the Lodge draws near, you need to be considering who will fill the position of Master of the Work (MOTW) or Ritual Instructor, and ensuring the Degree Captains understand their roles on the three Degree teams.

MAKE SURE THE INVESTIGATIVE COMMITTEE CHAIRMAN FOR THE CANDIDATE KNOWS TO CONTACT HIM ABOUT HIS DEGREE.

It is important that you begin this process now. Coordinate with the MOTW to let the members of the Lodge know what positions you would like them to fill; when, where and at what time the

Degree rehearsals will be, and when the Degrees are scheduled for presentation. Last minute preparation will go much smoother if you have a plan in place, and the Lodge members who will be assisting you in presenting the Degrees have plenty of time to prepare and learn their parts.

A candidate for your Lodge may have many opportunities to see and take part in Degree work in years to come, but they will only have one chance to be candidates. As candidates, there is much to learn from the Degrees; and the manner in which they are presented will, in great measure, determine just how much the candidates get out of the Degrees. Perfection is not required. Sincerity of purpose and reverence shown for that purpose is the desired goal.

DEGREE CAST SHEETS

Use this section for blank Degree Cast Sheets to use in planning degree work.

▢

TAB 11: ANNUAL OFFICIAL VISIT

Objective: To certify the ability of a Lodge to comply with the minimum standards for the basic conduct of Lodge meetings.

Process: A Lodge would be visited annually and asked to:

(1) Examine a visiting brother
(2) Ritualistic opening of the Lodge on any Degree
(3) Receive a Grand Lodge Officer
(4) Conduct a business meeting using one of the prescribed formats
(5) Conduct a ballot
(6) Ritualistic closing of the Lodge

▢

TAB 12: ANNUAL LODGE GOALS CHECKLIST

SPECIFIC GOALS FOR YOUR YEAR

(1) Raise a minimum of 1 brother per 30 members, with a minimum of 5 in Lodge, presenting all Degrees, including lectures

(2) Host a monthly Masonic Education program

(3) Assign a Mentor to every new brother

(4) Mentors are assigned for 1 year and each new brother is involved in a minimum of 2 Events

(5) Mentor assigned for 1 year, with records kept on tasks accomplished

(6) New brother is enrolled in University of Hiram and completes Bachelor level at minimum

(7) New Brother is issued In the Quarries Timecard and make satisfactory progress in ritual work

(8) Conduct a minimum of 1 program per year with appendant/concordant bodies

(9) Conduct a minimum of 1 evaluation per new brother within the first year of his mentorship and as a member of the Lodge

(10) The Lodge performs all Degree work by itself, including lectures

[?]

TAB 13: LODGE CALENDAR

Place your working calendar in this section.

[?]

TAB 14: GRAND LODGE ANNUAL COMMUNICATION

Place items pertaining to the Grand Lodge Annual Communication in this section.

[?]

TAB 15: STATE MASONIC CODE

Place Code copy in this section.

Degree Work

As Worshipful Master, you should now be relatively able to confer degrees and open and close your Lodge. Continually review what you have learned, but refrain from learning any additional parts of the degree work during this year. You job this year is to concentrate on and manage your Lodge, not learn the Stairway Lecture. Invest your time this year in the administrative, operational, and financial sectors of your Lodge. Continue to review your jurisdiction's Masonic Code Book, as you are charged primarily with protecting your Lodge's Charter.

If you do not know your Code, you cannot effectively protect your Charter.

Grand Lodge Leadership Directory

Name	Title	Phone

Degree Work as Worshipful Master

Date	Degree	Part	Lodge
3-1-13	MM	WM	Rockford Lodge No 469 F&AM

Candidate Tracking as Worshipful Master

Candidate Name	Phone Number	EA Date	FC Date	MM Date
John Smith	555-555-5555	*3-15-13*	*3-15-13*	*3-15-13*

Personal Notes as Worshipful Master

_____

_____

_____

_____

_____

_____

_____

_____

_____

_____

_____

_____

_____

_____

_____

_____

_____

_____

_____

Personal Notes as Worshipful Master

_____

_____

_____

_____

_____

_____

_____

_____

_____

_____

_____

_____

_____

_____

_____

_____

_____

_____

_____

Personal Notes as Worshipful Master

Personal Notes as Worshipful Master

Personal Notes as Worshipful Master

Personal Notes as Worshipful Master

NON-PROGRESSIVE LINE OFFICERS

8 THE TREASURER

The following officer does not usually move in the progressive line. Many times they have already progressed through all the chairs and choose to serve their lodge in different positions. Treasurers and Secretaries often serve their lodge in their respective positions for many years. Continuity in these positions is vital to a well-run and efficient lodge. Training takes time and if these officer positions changed each year, financial and accounting chaos would occur.

The Treasurer of a Masonic Lodge is the Chief Financial Officer of the Lodge. He sits to the right of the Master and behind the Senior Deacon. His Jewel is a Pair of Crossed Keys, signifying he is the Collector and Distributor of all Lodge Monies as he holds the keys to the cashbox.

The Treasurer is responsible for all financial transactions. He receives all money, pays all debts by order of the Worshipful Master with the consent of the lodge and renders a report when requested.

The treasurer does not need to be in possession of an accounting degree, however experience with bookkeeping and accounting is an asset.

Financial bookkeeping transactions may be performed either by hand or by the use of accounting software.

The Treasurer's duties are equivalent to a corporate C.F.O. (Chief Financial Officer) and is elected by the members of his Lodge.

Suggested Duties of the Treasurer

Check or fill in the Treasurer's Duties in your Lodge.

❑ Such duties as devolve by custom and usage or that shall be required by the Laws of the Grand Lodge or the By-Laws of the Lodge.

❑ Hold all deeds, certificates of stock, notes, bonds, obligations, or other property of a financial character, belonging to the Lodge, and to collect and receive the same when directed by the Lodge, to receive all monies from the hands of the Secretary, passing his receipt for the same, and pay them out only upon order of the Worshipful Master and consent of the Lodge.

❑ Keep a correct record of and report minutely the financial condition of the Lodge at the Stated Meeting next succeeding the festival of St. John the Evangelist (Dec. 27), and at such other times as the Lodge may direct.

❑ _____

_____

_____

❑ _____

_____

_____

Personal Notes as Treasurer

Personal Notes as Treasurer

9 THE SECRETARY

The following officer does not usually move in the progressive line. Many times they have already progressed through all the chairs and choose to serve their lodge in different positions. Treasurers and Secretaries often serve their lodge in their respective positions for many years. Continuity in these positions is vital to a well-run and efficient lodge. Training takes time and if these officer positions changed each year, financial and accounting chaos would occur.

His Jewel is the Crossed Quill Pens. The Secretary is the Lodge's Recorder. The Secretary's Lodge Officer Duties require a high degree of lodge experience, Masonic knowledge, diplomacy and, above all, detailed paperwork skills.

The Lodge Secretary is the backbone of any Masonic Lodge and he holds a position of great responsibility. He sits to the left of the Master. His duties require him to handle all correspondence to the members, minutes of Lodge meetings, petitions of new candidates, continuous lodge member count, and many other administrative duties.

He compiles an ongoing list of each new candidate and which degrees that candidate has undertaken. From his member list, he sends out the annual dues notices and receives dues payments. He communicates with other Lodges and the Grand Lodge, types letters, retrieves the mail as well as handles many other details.

The Secretary's Lodge Officer duties are many, not the least of which is that he must be well versed in Grand Lodge By-Laws for his jurisdiction and his Lodge By-Laws. He keeps the list of Lodge members and helps the Master organize his meetings.

A very experienced member usually resides in this chair...many times he is a Past Master of the Lodge. While it is not a prerequisite, due to the number of hours that this position requires, most (not all) Lodge Secretaries are retired and therefore able to devote the many hours required which are necessary to this position.

The Secretary's position is similar to a corporate C.O.O., (Chief Operation Officer), and he is elected by the members of his Lodge.

Suggested Duties of the Secretary

Check or fill in the Secretary's Duties in your Lodge.

❏ Such duties as devolve by custom and usage or that shall be required by the Laws of the Grand Lodge or the By-Laws of the Lodge.

❏ Make correct record of all things proper to be written pertaining to the business of the Lodge, collect all revenues of the Lodge and pay them over to the Treasurer, draw all warrants on the Treasurer, issue all summonses, Certificates of Demits, Certificates of Good Standing.

❏ It shall also be the duty of the Secretary to:

(1) Keep all books and papers relating to the proceedings of

the Lodge.

(2) Authenticate all official papers and documents emanating from the Lodge with the seal of the same.

(3) Notify all Brethren of their election to office, if they were not present at the time of election.

(4) Notify the Grand Secretary, as prescribed by law, of the suspension or expulsion of members, and of the rejection of applicants, to issue all summonses, demits, and notices as he may be directed, to make out and transmit to the Grand Secretary the monthly reports and annual returns of the Lodge, remit also the to him the Grand Lodge dues, report to the rand Secretary the names of all Brethren elected to Dual or Plural Membership, and perform all duties appertaining to his office.

❑ D. For his services he shall receive a salary to be decided upon by the Lodge at its first Stated Meeting of each Masonic year.

❑ E. Special Duties:

(1) Prepare or provide the resources to the appointed member, mailing labels of member names and addresses for quarterly communications mail outs.

(2) Provide the Communications Committee with updated Member and Widows contact information lists as needed for Lodge communications or events notification.

❑ _____

_____

_____

❑ _____

_____

Personal Notes as Secretary

Personal Notes as Secretary

Personal Notes as Secretary

_____

_____

_____

_____

_____

_____

_____

_____

_____

_____

_____

_____

_____

_____

_____

_____

_____

_____

10 THE CHAPLAIN

The following officer does not usually move in the progressive line. Many times they have already progressed through all the chairs and choose to serve their lodge in different positions. Continuity in these positions is vital to a well-run and efficient lodge.

The Chaplain of a Masonic Lodge is an appointed officer of the Lodge. He sits to the left of the Master. His Jewel of office is an opened book, symbolizing the Volume of Sacred Law (the Christian Bible, Hebrew Torah or Tanach, the Muslim Qur'an, the Hindu Vedas or other Holy Books), and he is the spiritual leader of the Lodge.

While he may or may not be a real-world Minister, Priest, Rabbi or Imam, ... in the lodge, the Chaplain is responsible for non-denominational prayers at both the opening and closing of meetings, during degree ritual ceremonies and before meals.

Most Chaplains have no religious training and prayers are non-denominational. The Chaplain's position is equivalent to that of a Supervisor.

Suggested Duties of the Chaplain

Check or fill in the Chaplain's Duties in your Lodge.

❑ Perform those solemn services which we constantly render to our Creator.

❑ Provide readings and Masonic interpretations of enlightened writings from the Supreme Architect of the Universe at Stated Meetings of the Lodge and at any occasion the Worshipful Master of the Lodge requests.

❑ Deliver the appropriate prayers at all Lodge meetings and gatherings.

❑ As a Masonic Scholar, serving as an avenue to further enlightenment of the brotherhood by availing himself to biblical inquiry, Masonic reference, and research questions concerning themselves with enlightened works.

❑ Devote a portion of his spare time to working on improving his knowledge of enlightened works and Masonic references contained therein.

❑ Keep a record of the readings and interpretations described in (B.), and at the end of his term of office, he will collect these works into a notebook, which shall be maintained in the Lodge Library.

❑ _____

_____

❑ _____

_____

Special Prayer as Chaplain

Date: _____ For:_____

Prayer:

_____

_____

_____

_____

_____

_____

_____

_____

_____

_____

_____

Special Prayer as Chaplain

Date: _____ For:_____

Prayer:

_____

_____

_____

_____

_____

_____

_____

_____

_____

_____

Special Prayer as Chaplain

Date: _____ For:_____

Prayer:

_____

_____

_____

_____

_____

_____

_____

_____

_____

_____

_____

Special Prayer as Chaplain

Date: _____ For:_____

Prayer:

_____

_____

_____

_____

_____

_____

_____

_____

_____

_____

_____

Special Prayer as Chaplain

Date: _____ For:_____

Prayer:

_____

_____

_____

_____

_____

_____

_____

_____

_____

_____

_____

Special Prayer as Chaplain

Date: _____ For:_____

Prayer:

_____

_____

_____

_____

_____

_____

_____

_____

_____

_____

_____

Special Prayer as Chaplain

Date: _____ For:_____

Prayer:

_____

_____

_____

_____

_____

_____

_____

_____

_____

_____

_____

_____

Special Prayer as Chaplain

Date: _____ For:_____

Prayer:

_____

_____

_____

_____

_____

_____

_____

_____

_____

_____

Special Prayer as Chaplain

Date: _____ For:_____

Prayer:

_____

_____

_____

_____

_____

_____

_____

_____

_____

_____

_____

Special Prayer as Chaplain

Date: _____ For:_____

Prayer:

_____

_____

_____

_____

_____

_____

_____

_____

_____

_____

Special Prayer as Chaplain

Date: _____ For:_____

Prayer:

_____

_____

_____

_____

_____

_____

_____

_____

_____

_____

Special Prayer as Chaplain

Date: _____ For:_____

Prayer:

_____

_____

_____

_____

_____

_____

_____

_____

_____

_____

Personal Notes as Chaplain

Personal Notes as Chaplain

_____

_____

_____

_____

_____

_____

_____

_____

_____

_____

_____

_____

_____

_____

_____

_____

_____

_____

11 THE MARSHAL

The following officer does not usually move in the progressive line. Many times they have already progressed through all the chairs and choose to serve their lodge in different positions. Continuity in these positions is vital to a well-run and efficient lodge.

The Marshal of a Masonic Lodge is an appointed officer of the Lodge. The Marshal is in some jurisdictions the "Director of Ceremonies". His Jewel of Office are the Crossed Batons. The Marshal is the Lodge's Conductor or Master of Ceremonies. The position may also differ from the Master of Ceremonies, depending on the Lodge.

The Marshal's duties and principle role is the organization of processions and ensuring the correct precedence and etiquette in formal proceedings. It is his duty to formally conduct visitors into the lodge and introduce them to the members when the lodge is in session. The Marshal's position is equivalent to that of a Supervisor.

Suggested Duties of the Marshal

Check or fill in the Marshal's Duties in your Lodge.

❑ Assist the Senior Deacon in preparing candidates for initiation and see that the needs of the candidate are provided, such as the New Member Handbook, Masonic Education and Information Program, Ritualistic Instruction, and the customs and uses of Masonry.

❑ He shall be responsible for the organization and presentation of any awards programs to the local school teachers and students, Lodge Parade Coordinator, Masonic Monument dedications and memorials, etc.. He will be supported by the Senior Deacon in this effort.

❑ _____

_____

_____

❑ _____

_____

_____

❑ _____

_____

_____

❑ _____

_____

_____

Record of Public Events Service as Marshal

Date   Event

_____   _____

_____   _____

_____   _____

_____   _____

_____   _____

_____   _____

_____   _____

_____   _____

_____   _____

_____   _____

_____   _____

_____   _____

_____   _____

_____   _____

_____   _____

_____   _____

Personal Notes as Marshal

_____

_____

_____

_____

_____

_____

_____

_____

_____

_____

_____

_____

_____

_____

_____

_____

_____

12 THE MASTER OF CEREMONIES

The following officer does not usually move in the progressive line. Many times they have already progressed through all the chairs and choose to serve their lodge in different positions. Continuity in these positions is vital to a well-run and efficient lodge.

The Master of Ceremonies of a Masonic Lodge is an appointed officer of the Lodge. The Master of Ceremonies is in some jurisdictions the "Director of Ceremonies". His Jewel of Office are the Crossed Batons. The Master of Ceremonies is the Lodge's Conductor or Master of Ceremonies. The position may also differ from the Master of Ceremonies, depending on the Lodge.

The Master of Ceremonies' duties and principle role is the organization of processions and ensuring the correct precedence and etiquette in formal proceedings. It is his duty to formally conduct visitors into the lodge and introduce them to the members when the lodge is in session. The Master of Ceremonies' position is equivalent to that of a Supervisor.

Suggested Duties of the Master of Ceremonies

Check or fill in the Master of Ceremonies' Duties in your Lodge.

❏ Assist the Senior Deacon in preparing candidates for initiation and see that the needs of the candidate are provided, such as the New Member Handbook, Masonic Education and Information Program, Ritualistic Instruction, and the customs and uses of Masonry.

❏ He shall be responsible for the organization and presentation of any awards programs to the local school teachers and students, Lodge Parade Coordinator, Masonic Monument dedications and memorials, etc.. He will be supported by the Senior Deacon in this effort.

❏ _____

_____

_____

❏ _____

_____

_____

❏ _____

_____

_____

❏ _____

_____

_____

Record of Public Events Service as MoC

Date   Event

_____   _____

_____   _____

_____   _____

_____   _____

_____   _____

_____   _____

_____   _____

_____   _____

_____   _____

_____   _____

_____   _____

_____   _____

_____   _____

_____   _____

_____   _____

_____   _____

Personal Notes as Master of Ceremonies

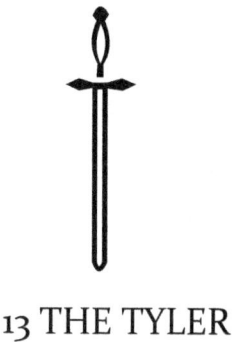

13 THE TYLER

The following officer does not usually move in the progressive line. Many times they have already progressed through all the chairs and choose to serve their lodge in different positions. Continuity in these positions is vital to a well-run and efficient lodge.

The Tyler of a Masonic Lodge is an appointed officer of the Lodge and is sometimes known as the "Outer Guard". He sits outside the closed door of the lodge room, armed with a sword. The Tyler's duties and principle role is to ensure that only those who are duly qualified are allowed to enter the Lodge Room.

His Jewel of Office is the Sword, by which he symbolically refuses entrance to anyone who is uninitiated in the Craft. The sword has no scabbard, as it is his symbolic duty to always have his sword drawn, ready for the defense of his post.

He guards against cowans and eavesdroppers. During the Middle Ages, a cowan was a man who built stone walls of poor quality. He was an uninitiated or non-apprenticed stonemason...a "jackleg", if you will.

While the Tyler is sometimes called upon to assist in the

preparation of candidates, his chief duty is to (symbolically) keep unskilled workmen from overhearing the conversation within the Lodge Room.

After the lodge members are inside the Lodge Room, the door closes and it is the Tyler's duty to decide whether late arrivals may enter. It is also his duty to make sure that each visitor is "properly clothed", which means they must be wearing their Masonic apron.

To be fully and properly dressed before entrance into the Lodge Room, the visitor must be wearing their apron over the top (or on the outside) of their suit coat (never under their coat) and the apron strings must be fully tied before the Tyler will allow the visitor entrance. Some jurisdictions call this position the Outer Guard.

The Tyler's position is similar to that of a Supervisor.

Suggested Duties of the Tyler

Check or fill in the Master of Ceremonies' Duties in your Lodge.

❑ See that the Lodge Room is kept clean and in order, and that the various articles of furniture are in their appropriate places; strictly guard the door during the sitting of the Lodge; summon the members of the Lodge to all called meetings where a summons is necessary, and be punctual in attendance.

❑ When the Grand Master (or other such officials, as the case may be) shall arrive in the anteroom, the Tyler shall give the alarm and announce that the Grand Master (or his representative) is in waiting.

❑ Guard against the approach of cowans and eavesdroppers, and permit none to pass except those who are duly qualified.

❑ Set up the Lodge before every Stated and Called Meeting.

This includes the proper articles at each station and appropriate articles placed within the Lodge for degree work.

❏ After the close of each Lodge function, it is the duty of the Tyler to insure that the Lodge is secure, the lights and HVAC set to the appropriate settings, and the doors locked. If the Tyler is unable to perform this function, it will be his responsibility to arrange for another Brother to perform this function and inform both the Worshipful Master and the Secretary of this temporary change of responsibility.

❏ The duties of the Tyler shall include, but are not limited to:

❏ Guard against the intrusion of cowans and eavesdroppers and admit visitors if properly vouched for and clothed.

❏ Ensure the aprons are laid out prior to the arrival of the Brethren and neatly put away after the Brethren leave.

❏ Ensure all soiled aprons are clean before storage.

❏ Ensure that the video monitoring system, if any, is in proper working order.
❏
E. Clean the anteroom before each meeting, to include the emptying the ash trays.

❏ Be proficient in the Tyler's Oath and examining Visitors.

❏ _____

_____

_____

❏ _____

_____

_____

Personal Notes as Tyler

_____

_____

_____

_____

_____

_____

_____

_____

_____

_____

_____

_____

_____

_____

_____

_____

Personal Notes as Tyler

SPECIALLY-APPOINTED OFFICERS

14 THE MASTER OF THE WORK (RITUALIST)

The following officer does not usually move in the progressive line. Many times they have already progressed through all the chairs and choose to serve their lodge in different positions. Continuity in these positions is vital to a well-run and efficient lodge.

The Master of the Work was the operative Mason in charge of the training and supervision of workmen in the Middle Ages.

He is appointed as a special officer by the Worshipful Master to assist with the training and education of the Lodge in the ritual work of Masonry.

His Jewel is the Past Master's Symbol. The Master of the Work is the Lodge's Ritual Instructor, and supervises the training of members in the ritual practice and performance of duties in the degree work.

Suggested Duties of the Master of the Work

Check or fill in the Master of the Work's Duties in your Lodge.

A. To ensure a program of education and instruction is developed and maintained within the Lodge.

B. To oversee the conduct and operation of Lodge ritual practice meetings.

C. To coordinate with the Degree Captains on the conferral or exemplification of degree work within the Lodge.

D. To assist the Lodge Master Educator with Masonic Education duties as needed or required.

E. To perform any other duties as specified by the Grand Lodge or Grand Lecturer pertaining to ritual instruction.

F. To serve as the Lodge liaison between the Grand Lodge Committee on Work, the Grand Lecturer, and the Worshipful Master.

G. To keep the Lodge abreast of any change, additions, or deletions of ritual work in the jurisdiction.

❏ _____

_____

_____

❏ _____

_____

_____

Personal Notes as Master of the Work

Personal Notes as Master of the Work

_____

_____

_____

_____

_____

_____

_____

_____

_____

_____

_____

_____

_____

_____

_____

_____

_____

_____

15 THE MASTER EDUCATOR (LEO)

The following officer does not usually move in the progressive line. Many times they have already progressed through all the chairs and choose to serve their lodge in different positions. Continuity in these positions is vital to a well-run and efficient lodge.

The Master Educator was the operative Mason in charge of the training and education of workmen in the Trivium and Quadrivium (Seven Liberal Arts and Sciences) during the Middle Ages.

He is appointed as a special officer by the Worshipful Master to assist with the training and education of the Lodge in Masonic Education.

His Jewel is the Past Master's Symbol. The Master Educator is the Lodge's Masonic Education Instructor, and supervises the training of members in the history, practices and meaning of Masonry.

Suggested Duties of the Master Educator

Check or fill in the Master Educator's Duties in your Lodge.

A. To ensure a program of Masonic education and instruction is developed and maintained within the Lodge.

B. To oversee the conduct and operation of Lodge Masonic education meetings.

C. To coordinate with the members of the Lodge on an Masonic education events or opportunities within the Lodge's District.

D. To assist the Lodge Master of the Work with Ritual Instruction duties as needed or required.

E. To perform any other duties as specified by the Grand Lodge pertaining to Masonic education and instruction.

F. To serve as the Lodge liaison between the Grand Lodge Education Committee and the Worshipful Master.

G. To keep the Lodge abreast of any updates or opportunities in Masonic Education within the jurisdiction.

❑ _____

_____

_____

❑ _____

_____

_____

Personal Notes as Master Educator

Personal Notes as Master Educator

_____

_____

_____

_____

_____

_____

_____

_____

_____

_____

_____

_____

_____

_____

_____

_____

_____

_____

_____

ABOUT THE AUTHOR

The Author, Bro. James Frank Hatcher III, better known as "Chip," is a Master Mason and Past Worshipful Master of Rockford Masonic Lodge No. 469, Free and Accepted Masons of Tennessee, in Rockford, Tennessee ~ a small, quiet hamlet in the foothills of the Great Smoky Mountains in Eastern Tennessee. He lives with his wife, three children, three dogs, six cats, two hermit crabs, and nearby to many, many wonderful friends, whom he later found to be his Brothers in many, many different situations.

He is also the Author of the:

Worshipful Master's Guidebook, or the "Book of Joe."
https://www.createspace.com/4523383

and

King Solomon's Passport
https://www.createspace.com/4531237

SO·MOTE·IT·BE

www.ingramcontent.com/pod-product-compliance
Lightning Source LLC
Chambersburg PA
CBHW070852290526
45795CB00001B/85